CARING FOR YOUR PET BIRD

Dedicated to
my wife Judy for her understanding
and patience during the many months
required to write this book

Dr. R. Dean Axelson

CARING FOR YOUR PET BIRD

Sterling Publishing Co., Inc. New York

Library of Congress Cataloging-in-Publication Data
Axelson, R. Dean.
Caring for your pet bird.
Bibliography: p.
Includes index.
1. Cage Birds. I. Title.
SF461.A94 1989 636.6'86 88-32775
ISBN 0-8069-6986-5

1 3 5 7 9 10 8 6 4 2

Published in 1989 by Sterling Publishing Co., Inc.
Two Park Avenue, New York, N.Y. 10016

Distributed in Canada by Oak Tree Press Ltd.
% Canadian Manda Group, P.O. Box 920, Station U
Toronto, Ontario, Canada M8Z 5P9
Distributed in Great Britain and Europe by Cassell PLC
Artillery House, Artillery Row, London SW1P 1RT, England
Distributed in Australia by Capricorn Ltd.
P.O. Box 665, Lane Cove, NSW 2066
Manufactured in the United States of America

Sterling ISBN 0-8069-6986-5 Paper

Contents

Acknowledgements

This book could not have been produced without the help and goodwill of my friends and fellow professionals. I wish to thank: my wife and family for their support; the many friends who helped me with the photography; Dr. Theodore J. Lafeber, DVM whose own writings on pet bird care encouraged me to begin this book; Dr. Margaret L. Petrak, VMD and her publisher, Lea & Febiger, for reference material and reprint permission; Kathy Lyon and *Bird World* magazine for her support and the magazine's permission to reprint selected material; Dr. William Alfred Rapley, DVM for his critical reading and appraisal of the final text, and Melinda M. Leal and Applied Imagery Inc. for editorial and production guidance.

The publishers would like to thank the following for permission to reproduce colour photographs: Aquila Photographics (M. Gilroy), Plate 1; Alan Beaumont, Plates 4, 6, 8, 10, 14.

Preface

In my practice I am continually asked very basic questions about the birds my clients keep as pets and companions. This fundamental lack of understanding about birds prompts many clients to ask, "where can I find one book that gathers all of this information together?" In fact, there are a lot of quality books about birds on the market, but much of the information they offer is either too slanted to one species, too specialized, or just too scientific. The need for a simple "how to" book is what urged me to write this handy reference on the day-to-day care of pet birds. There are certain fundamental principles, insights and truths that hold for all birds, and owners should be aware of these, whether their pet is a budgie or a scarlet macaw.

Owning a pet bird is a pleasure, but it is also a serious responsibility. A pet bird is totally dependent on its owner for whatever care, comfort and sustenance it requires. Your bird needs you, and in turn, more and more people are being attracted to the idea of owning a bird.

Birds fill a great need in people's lives. A bird can bring all of nature into your home with its song and beauty. Besides being relatively easy to care for, birds give their owners affection, warmth and entertainment, particularly to those people who could not otherwise have a pet because of spatial or housing restrictions. Whether home is an apartment or full-sized house, we all need something there, warm and cheery, to greet us after a hard day's work. Birds bring this kind of cheer into people's lives. They can also become a fascinating hobby for owners who want to go further with their birds: raising or breeding them, and even showing them competitively.

In the following pages, my purpose is to lay out the various aspects of bird care, so that you can learn how to create a suitable environment for your bird, care for most of its needs yourself, feed it wisely and handle it with confidence. In coming to understand what is needed to keep your bird healthy and happy, you will be assured of enjoying your pet to the fullest.

The second portion of this book gathers together selected reading materials on bird diets and bird behaviour. It also contains some helpful information on rescue work with wild birds – for those readers whose love of birds knows no bounds. Those of you who wish to go more deeply into particular topics or species that I mention may find the section on Further Reading, also in Part II, of some help in guiding you to the books you seek.

Dr. R. Dean Axelson

PART I
Introduction

ANATOMY AND PHYSIOLOGY

The anatomy or physical structure of birds is different from that of mammals, as they are designed to be able to fly. They are lighter in proportion to size, are streamlined, and have air sacs which connect into

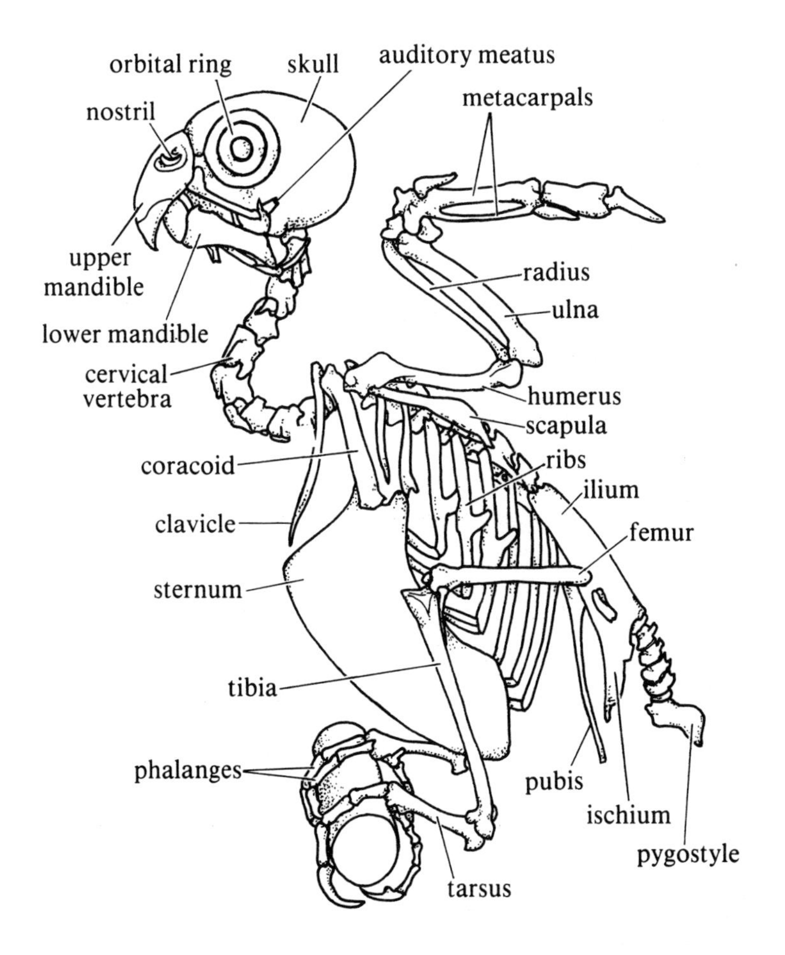

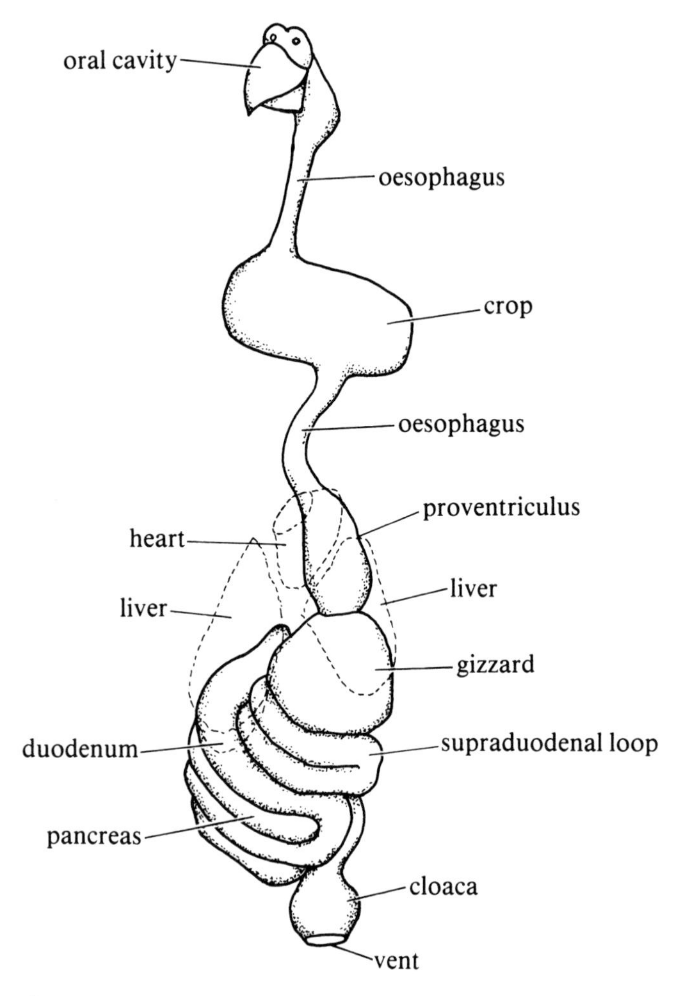

The digestive tract.

some of their bones and body cavity in order to make their respiratory system more efficient. They have a beak that is designed to meet the requirements of the diet they eat. Seed eaters have heavier beaks than insect eaters, and meat eaters have special beaks to tear the flesh of their prey. The feet and legs of birds vary depending also on how they are used. Birds that run on the ground have stronger legs and feet than perching birds. Psittacine birds have two toes forward and two toes facing rearward to allow them to climb better and hold their food while they eat. Birds that prey on animals or other birds have strong, well-developed legs and feet with long talons which they use to catch their prey. They also have an outer covering of feathers instead of hair to maintain body temperature.

The digestive tract of birds is also designed to be lighter by being shorter. They cannot store as much food in their stomachs at one meal as a mammal can as the weight would interfere with flying. Therefore they have to eat more frequently. They have a dilatation of the oesophagus positioned just before the inlet into the thoracic cavity, which is a food storage area called the crop. When a bird eats, the food is temporarily stored in the crop and from there it passes down into the proventriculus where digestive juices are added and the digestive process begins. From there the food passes into the gizzard which is a very muscular organ. Here the food is ground up with the aid of the gravel or grit that the bird has eaten plus the contractions of the muscular gizzard. This grit takes the place of teeth which are absent in birds. The gizzard is more developed and muscular in some species than others, depending on their diet. The proventriculus and the gizzard (ventriculus), are both considered to be parts of a bird's stomach. The duodenum is the first part of the intestinal tract and here further digestive enzymes are added from the pancreas and liver. Digestion continues as the food passes down the intestinal tract and nutrients are absorbed through the intestinal wall where the blood supply transports it to the rest of the body.

Waste products are passed down to the cloaca which is a communal collecting area at the rear end of the digestive tract. The cloaca is also a collecting pot for the excretions coming from the kidneys and urinary tract which is often in the form of white urate crystals or excess water (urine). The reproductive tract of both sexes exits into the cloaca as well. From the

The excretory organs.

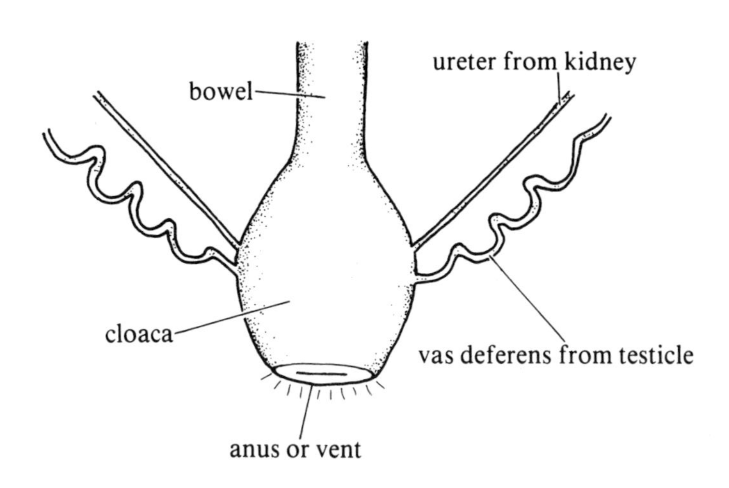

cloaca, the body waste is excreted out of the body in the form of the dropping that all bird owners are familiar with.

The respiratory system of birds has been modified by the addition of air sacs which enlarge the air holding capacity of the lungs. These air sacs are fibrous walled pouches that extend into parts of the thoracic cavity, abdominal cavity, and the humerus or first long bone of each wing. On inhalation, air fills the lungs and air sacs. On expiration, the air escapes back out through the lungs where it carries away waste carbon dioxide and oxygen is left behind by being absorbed by the blood supply in the lung tissue. These air sacs also make a bird lighter in weight.

There is no diaphragm or muscular flap present between the chest cavity and abdominal cavity in birds as there is in mammals which aids mammals to breathe easier. Birds breathe by expansion and contraction of the chest wall only.

Birds have a very heavy development of muscles on their chest (called pectoral muscles), which are important in the process of flying. A healthy active bird will have a well developed chest muscle area on both sides of the sternum. These muscles atrophy or shrink in size quickly when a bird is not eating properly and maintaining its weight. A protruding sternum or keel bone means a thin bird and possibly a sick bird. Pectoral muscles are generally the heaviest muscle mass on most birds and are the site of choice for intramuscular injections when treating sick birds.

1
The Cage Environment

A bird is literally the captive of his cage environment. He has brought nothing to this environment save his health, and therefore it is up to you to supply everything else he needs to carry on a healthy, active and well-adjusted existence.

CAGE SIZE

The desire to fly, both for exercise and self-expression, is fundamental to birds. Whether this be from perch to perch, or from one end of the cage to another, the bird must have enough room to manoeuvre with ease. A cage that is longer in either its width or length is better than one of more squared dimensions. Similarly, rectangular cages are preferable to round ones. The bird should be able to stretch his wings (clipped or unclipped), and flap them for exercise without touching the sides of the cage. Birds love to flap their wings and will become unhappy if they cannot do this.

The tall, narrow type of cage is quite impractical. It may look attractive, but it means very poor housing for any bird. It compares to a person living in an elevator shaft, and, besides, birds do not fly straight up and down. The greater length of a cage allows more room for flying and exercising.

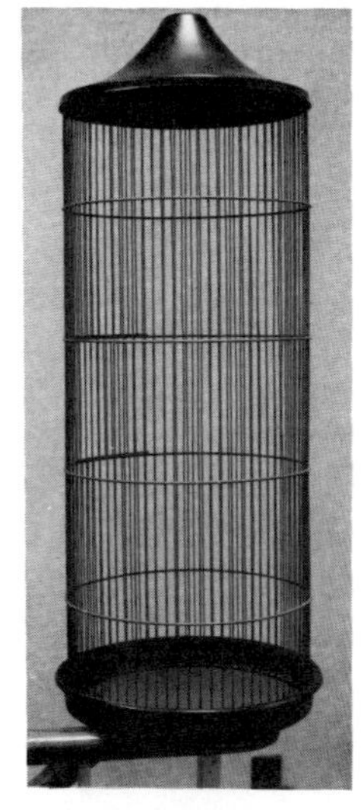

Too tall, too narrow.

Rectangular is ideal: its greater length gives flying room.

Recommended Minimum Cage Sizes		
Approximate Bird Size	**Minimum Cage Size**	**Dimensions**
Finch, Canary, Budgie	2 cubic feet	1′ × 1′ × 2′
Cockatiel, Love Bird	12 cubic feet	2′ × 2′ × 3′
Small Parrots	18 cubic feet	2′ × 3′ × 3′
Larger Parrots	24 cubic feet	2′ × 3′ × 4′
Macaws	32 cubic feet	2′ × 4′ × 4′

CAGE TYPES

Anyone who steps into a pet shop may leave with the impression that there are as many cage shapes as there are birds. But the majority of these cages are variations on two basic designs.

The most popular design has wire all round, and gives an unobstructed view of the bird. Certainly this type has great appeal to the owner, but from the bird's point of view, it means complete exposure to draughts, noise or whatever happens by[1]. These all-wire cages should be thoughtfully placed in a relatively quiet, draught-free area, and I heartily recommend covering one side of the cage so that the bird feels somewhat protected from disturbances.

Commercial cages of the sort described above sometimes run to the ornamental, and are better suited to interior decorating than they are to the needs of a bird. Manufacturers produce designs for every taste: from wicker shapes and bamboo pagodas to french provincial and modern pine. The more elaborate these fashionable objects become, the more difficult they are to clean. Some actually epitomize the worst cage conditions a bird could endure. A bird's cage should be selected for its functional value. Its size must fit the bird's needs, while the materials used in its construction must be durable enough to withstand frequent cleaning and disinfecting.

The second type of cage, the box cage, is a very practical design for birds. It is made of solid material, and has either wood or metal on three sides. The open front portion has wire mesh or bars. This type of cage reduces the danger of draughts, and provides the bird with security and privacy[2]. It is simple to construct, but the inside must be either left unpainted or else

1. William C. Dilger, "Caging and Environment," in *Diseases of Cage and Aviary Birds*, ed. Margaret L. Petrak, V.M.D. (Philadelphia: Lea & Febiger, 1969), p. 13.
2. Ibid.

Pretty is not always practical.

Box cage. Note the sliding tray, which is for cleaning purposes.

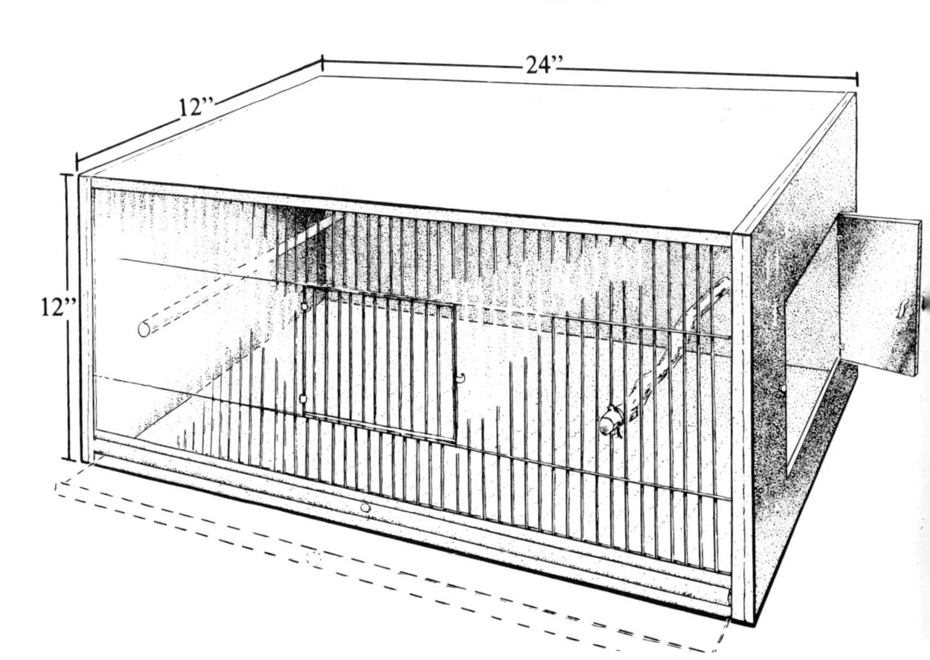

painted with a non-toxic paint such as that used on baby toys and furniture. The top and one side can also be covered with wire to create a "semi-box cage" that gives the bird more visibility. Generally, box cages are not available commercially and have to be homemade.

Build your cage, or obtain one, with wire openings small enough that the bird cannot put his head through the bars. This is very important. More birds have been lost in this way than in almost any other cage accident. When a bird gets his head stuck between the bars in his cage, he is likely to panic, and then die of fright or a broken neck.

CAGE DANGERS

Improperly latched cage doors may allow a bird to escape, and then be lost through an open door or window. When your bird is in its cage, be sure the door is fastened shut.

Watch for sharp objects or things that project into the cage and remove or cover these, so as not to injure your bird. Broken wires, wood splinters, plastic splinters, metal shavings or nails are among these common hazards.

Sometimes birds get caught up in wires or cords used to hang various things inside their cage, or they become the hapless victims of lead poisoning. They may be tempted to chew on electrical wires that are close-by, or to eat bits of lead-based paint. Remember that only lead-free paint should be used on the cage. Find a safe place for your bird's cage, keep it in good repair, and watch carefully to prevent situations arising that might injure your bird.

T-BAR STANDS

Pet shops sell these floor stands. They consist of an upright pole with a horizontal perch across the top in the shape of a "T". Called T-Bar perches, these stands usually have a food and water cup at either end of the cross bar, and a large circular tray underneath to catch the food debris and droppings.

When used as a temporary release from the bird's cage, or as an exercise area, these stands are quite valuable. But if the bird is forced to remain there for prolonged periods, the stand becomes a very poor environment, harmful to the bird's physical and psychological well-being. Over long

For large birds, the T-Bar stand can be a welcome change from their everyday cage.

periods the T-Bar stands become confining and boring. They offer no privacy and will soon drive a bird into a poor state of mental health, which in turn can lead to psychological problems like feather-picking.

A very appealing exercise area can be created by attaching a series of climbing bars to the top of the bird's cage. These bars are of great benefit to psittacine birds like parrots and cockatiels. When let out of their cage, they will get both exercise and entertainment from climbing up and down these bars.

PERCHES

A bird spends most of its time standing on a perch, so the right perch arrangements are very important. "Perches should be placed at the same height and as far apart as possible[3]." Allow enough clearance between the perch and the end of the cage that the bird can turn freely and not damage his tail feathers from constant rubbing. Try to arrange the perches so that a low-sitting bird or lower perch will not be defaecated on by the bird on a higher perch[4]. And remember to place the perches so they can be easily removed for cleaning.

Tree branches or twigs make the best perches. If you want to supply your bird with natural perches "cut [them] from non-toxic trees and shrubs, such as fruit trees, or elm, ash, maple, willow, and nut trees[5]". Cherry tree bark may be toxic, so do not use this type. The natural perches are better because of their different diameter and the ease with which birds can grasp them. The different diameters give the feet better exercise. Chewing on these branches also provides beak exercise and some bonus nutrition from the bark.

Before placing natural perches in the cage, wash the branches thoroughly, but leave the bark on. Be careful that branches do not have narrow "V" shaped angles where they join a heavier part of the branch; these acute angles may catch legs or necks and cause injury. Natural perches are more difficult to clean, but they can be scrubbed and replaced often. Commercial perches can be cleaned by scrubbing with soap and water, and rubbing them down afterward with a coarse sandpaper.

Various perch shapes such as flat, oval, or rectangular (when viewed in cross section) will help ease the stress load on the feet and reduce the incidence of pressure sores. But, in my experience, the most common cause of foot soreness is the sandpaper coverings that are designed to slip around the perch. These coverings are of dubious value. They do little to help wear down the nails, and much to irritate the bottoms of the feet by wearing off

---

3. Dilger, p. 12.
4. Ibid.
5. Ibid.

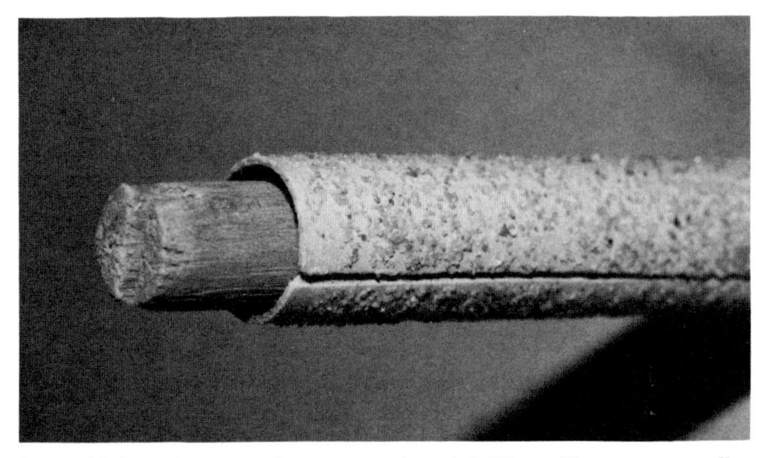

Making a bird stand on a sandpaper-covered perch is like making someone walk on a gravel road in bare feet.

the skin of tender-footed species. Making a bird stand on a sandpaper-covered perch is comparable to making someone walk on a gravel road in bare feet.

At least one soft perch in the cage is advisable in order to help the feet stay healthy. Any perch can be padded by wrapping it in some soft fabric, or the soft perch itself can be made of plastic or rubber hose.

FOOD AND WATER DISHES

These should be made from a sturdy, non-toxic material that is easily cleaned and disinfected. If the dishes are to be used by a larger bird,

Look for food and water dishes that are sturdy, and easy to clean.

especially one of the psittacine (parrot) family, they must also be made from materials the bird cannot chew apart. Containers with hard to clean corners, crevices, or cracks should be avoided.

Food and water dishes often get contaminated with droppings and dust, so they must be kept clean. Wash and clean the cups every day, and soak them weekly in a disinfecting quaternary ammonium solution. Rinse the dishes well afterward. If you have two sets of dishes, rotating these will allow you more time for cleaning and disinfecting. (A quick, easy way to wash the dishes is by automatic dishwasher, if you own one.)

Place the dishes in the cage so that they are easily reached for cleaning, and quite available to the bird, but will not be unduly contaminated by his droppings.

DAY TO DAY CARE

A dirty cage can create a sick bird. Regardless of the type of cage used, it is very important to keep your bird's house clean and free of germs. For instance, his cage should be cleaned daily. In order to make this job as convenient as possible, is is best to spread paper of some sort on the cage floor. Although paper towelling is becoming more costly, it remains a favourite for this purpose. White paper or plain newspaper is still inexpensive, easy to obtain and can be used with perfect safety.

Newspaper is not harmful to birds. Even though there is a small amount of lead in the printers' ink, a small bird would have to eat a whole page of editorial to be in any danger[6]. However, do be cautious about the use of "gravel paper" on the bottom of the cage; its use is not advised. This sandpaper-like substance actually irritates the feet. Nor is there much value in pouring gravel or grit all over the cage floor. The loose mixture becomes messy, and is no substitute for a proper grit-mineral supplement[7].

Paper is the best solution. By cutting several sheets to the size and shape of the cage bottom, it becomes a very simple task eash day to remove the top sheet of droppings and seed husks. Changing these papers daily gets rid of any bacterial growth, and helps you keep a close eye on the health of your bird. Frequent changes prevent the accumulation of bird waste, which dries to a powdery material, full of bacteria, that can be blown into the bird's food, its water dishes and the very air it breathes.

A bird's droppings are a good indicator of its state of health. By checking the number and consistency of each day's excretions, you can tell whether or not a bird is eating properly and passing normal droppings. This is best viewed on a white paper background.

---

6. T.J. Lafeber, D.V.M., *Tender Loving Care For Pet Birds* (Park Ridge, Illinois: Dorothy Products, 1977), p. 23.
7. Wood shavings and kitty litter should not be used on the cage bottom either. Some birds, particularly young ones, may eat this material, and then experience severe bowel blockage and death.

WASHING & DISINFECTING

Your regular routine of changing the bird's paper will also include a thorough cleaning of his cage once a week. If you are keeping more than one bird, or have an aviary, this practice is even more important. Disease can be spread among a group of birds very easily if they live in a dirty environment.

Give the cage a good scrub each week.

The removal of dirt, dust and faecal matter is of primary importance. Each week, the whole cage should be scrubbed down with soap, hot water and a sturdy brush. Food and water dishes should also be soaked in a good disinfectant, and a spare set returned to the cage.

A thorough disinfecting job is done on the cage and its contents at least every two weeks. The disinfectant will kill bacteria and any other organisms, like fungi and viruses, which cause disease.

After a good scrub, soak the items in disinfectant for at least thirty minutes, then rinse well in plain water and allow to dry, preferably in the sun. If you have a lot of birds and cleaning to do, use plastic garbage pails to put your wash water, disinfectant and rinse water in.

Remember that porous materials such as wood, bamboo and wicker are next to impossible to sterilize. Germs and dirt penetrate them too deeply. These materials are strictly decorative and should not be made into things, such as bird cages, which require constant cleaning and disinfecting.

In your own construction of cages or aviaries try to use only non-porous materials like metal, masonite, tile, plastic, cement or glass. Wood must be used for some things – perches, nest boxes and so forth – but these should be replaced yearly. The floors of aviaries or bird rooms are best surfaced with a smoothly finished cement that can be easily washed and disinfected.

THE RANGE OF DISINFECTANTS

There are several different kinds of disinfectants that you can use. Some are capable of killing all forms of germs (viruses, bacteria, fungi), while others are specifically formulated to act only on certain types of germs.

If you have an aviary, or a large number of birds, you are better off using a broad range disinfectant to control the spread of bacteria. For a small bird in a single cage, a general disinfectant-deodorizer is adequate.

The following is a list of disinfectants that are relatively easy to find. Some are available in grocery, drug and hardware stores, but others can only be purchased at janitorial supply companies. Each one will, if used according to the manufacturer's instructions, keep the cage clean and germ free.

Phenol Derivatives are very strong disinfectants. The active ingredient, phenol, is corrosive to skin and special care should be taken with its use. Wear protective rubber gloves, keep it away from your eyes, and follow the manufacturer's directions carefully.

KEM 77TM. This liquid disinfectant-deodorizer combination is effective against a wide range of microorganisms. As a general disinfectant, use 60–125 ml/litre of water. Manufactured by Kem manufacturing Canada Ltd., Mississauga, Ontario.

2004 DETERGENT-GERMICIDETM. This disinfectant contains synthetic phenols in liquid form. It is effective against a wide range of microorganisms. As a general disinfectant, use 25 ml/litre of water. Manufactured by G.H. Wood Ltd., Toronto, Ontario.

DETTOLTM is another liquid disinfectant-deodorizer that is quite effective in killing bacteria. Use 80–90 ml/litre. Manufactured by Reckitt & Colman, Canada, Inc., Lachine, Quebec.

ASEPTOTM VETERINARY DISINFECTANT SPRAY. This spray is highly virucidal and has good activity against other microorganisms as well. Spray on after surfaces have been cleaned. Manufactured by Becton-Dickinson, Rutherford, New Jersey, 07070, USA.

1 STROKE ENVIRONTM. A potent germicidal, fungicidal and virucidal agent. Follow the directions on the container. It is made by Ceva Laboratories, 10560 Barkely Street, Overland Park, Kansas, 66212, USA.

STAPHENETM DISINFECTANT SPRAY AND AIR SANITIZER. This product is germicidal, fungicidal, and eliminates many viruses as well as being a deodorizer. Directions for use are on the container, and it is made by Vestal Laboratories, Div. Chemed Corporation, St. Louis, Missouri, 63110, USA.

Quaternary Ammonium disinfectants are reasonably effective if used on clean surfaces. They are usually available through janitorial supply outlets.

ROCCAL DTM is a fairly strong disinfectant. Recommended dilution: 2 ml/litre of water. Manufactured by Winthrop Laboratories, Division of Sterling Drug Ltd., Aurora, Ontario.

QUATSYL DTM. This product is made primarily for veterinary hospitals, but would be effective in bird rooms as well. It is a disinfectant-deodorizer in detergent form, comparable to Roccal DTM. Recommended dilution: 10 ml/litre of water. Manufactured by

Winthrop Laboratories, Division of Sterling Drug Ltd., Aurora, Ontario.
CLEAR-LEMON-10TM is a lemon scented germicide and deodorizer. Recommended dilution: 20 ml/litre of water. Manufactured by Paragon Laboratories Inc., Great Neck, New York.
TRL-02 TRI SANTM. This is a liquid germicidal cleaner that kills a wide range of microorganisms. Recommended dilution: 16 ml/litre of water. Manufactured by Trojan Chemicals Ltd., Rexdale, Ontario.

Iodine based products use iodine as the germicidal agent, and are quite effective against a wide range of germs. Some of these products will stain.

WELADOL DISINFECTANTTM is a bactericidal, virucidal and fungicidal liquid disinfectant. Recommended dilution: 2 ml/litre of water. Manufactured by Pitman-Moore, Inc., Washington Crossing, New Jersey.

Chlorine bleach agents, like JavexTM, are fairly effective in killing bacteria and other disease organisms. JavexTM contains sodium hypochlorate which releases chlorine, the killing agent. Mix about 50 ml/litre of water. Soak all items for a minimum of thirty minutes. Manufactured by Bristol-Myers Canada Inc., Toronto, Ontario.
Manufacturers' Brands: A number of manufacturers have formulated their own disinfectants to meet specific institutional needs.

HIBITANE DISINFECTANTTM is a bactericidal, fungicidal and virucidal agent. Recommended dilution: 25 ml/litre of water. Manufactured by Ayerst Laboratories. Montreal, Quebec. Sold in USA under name of NOLVASANTM by Fort Dodge Laboratories, Inco, Fort Dodge, Iowa, 50501. Active ingredient is chlorhexidine.
SAVLON HOSPITAL CONCENTRATETM is a broad spectrum bactericidal agent with detergent action. Recommended dilution: 7 ml/litre of water. Manufactured by Ayerst Laboratories, Montreal, Quebec.
ZEPHIRAN CHLORIDETM is a fairly effective disinfectant. Recommended dilution: 2 ml/litre of water. Manufactured by Winthrop Laboratories, Division of Sterling Drug Ltd., Aurora, Ontario.
VANODINE is widely used in aviaries. Manufactured by Vanodine International Ltd., Chadwick Rd., Eccles, Salford, Manchester, UK.
CIDEX 7TM STERILIZING AND DISINFECTING SOLUTION. This product is a formaldehyde origin product and is virucidal, bactericidal, fungicidal and sporicidal. The directions for use should be followed carefully. It is made by Arbrook, Inc., Arlington, Texas, 76010, USA.

2
The Home Environment

A bird's house is his cage, and his home is the greater environment within your home. For a happy, healthy bird, certain conditions need to be met in this greater environment to ensure the bird's safety and well-being.

TEMPERATURE AND HUMIDITY

Normally, because of the insulating quality of his feathers, a bird can tolerate moderate changes in the environmental temperature and humidity. Providing he is not in a draught, a healthy bird can withstand a 10–20°(F) degree fluctuation in the ambient temperature, but a sick bird will be adversely affected by this change. A humidity reading of 40–50% creates the ideal condition for your bird. Birds adapt more easily to excess humidity (readings greater than 50%) than to dryness, although they can tolerate humidity readings as low as 25–30%, except when they are breeding.

Generally, healthy birds do quite well in a moderately warm and not too humid environment, as long as they are free from draughts.

Do not place your bird anywhere near a hot or cold window, air vent or radiator. If allowed to sun themselves, birds must have access to some form of shade because direct sunlight on a hot summer's day will quickly produce heat stroke and death. Cold outside walls, especially stone or brick walls that are poorly insulated, may radiate a cold draught in the wintertime and be dangerous for your bird.

SOME OF THE MORE COMMON POTENTIALLY POISONOUS PLANTS

No controlled research experimentation has been done on birds by feeding them plants listed here as "potentially" poisonous. This list was compiled from plants known to be poisonous or harmful to mammals. Birds may be able to tolerate more of the toxins in these plants than mammals can, but if you feed your birds any plants listed here, you do so at your own risk.

HOUSE PLANTS	*SCIENTIFIC NAME*
Amaryllis	*Amaryllis* spp.
Autumn Crocus (*Meadow Saffron)	*Colchicum* spp.

Azalea	*Azalea* spp.
Balsam Pear	*Memordica charantia*
Bird of Paradise	*Poinciana gilliesii*
Boxwood	*Buxus* spp.
Caladium	*Caladium* spp.
Castor Bean (*Castor Oil Plant)	*Ricinus communis*
Chalice Vine	*Solandra* spp.
Coral Plant	*Jatropha multifida*
Daffodil	*Narcissus* spp.
Datura (berries)	*Datura* spp.
Dieffenbachia	*Dieffenbachia picta*
Egg-Plant (all except fruit)	Nightshade family (Solanaceae)
Elephant's Ear (*Taro)	*Colocasia* spp.
Hyacinth	*Galtonia* spp.
Hydrangea	*Hydrangea macrophylla*
Japanese Yew	*Taxus cuspidata*
Java Beans (*Glorybean)	*Phaseolus lunatus* (variety of)
Lantana	*Lantana* spp.
Lily-Of-The-Valley	*Convallaria majalis*
Narcissus	*Narcissus* spp.
Nightshade (Deadly, black, Garden or Woody Nightshade)	Solanaceae
Oleander	*Nerium* spp.
Philodendron	*Philodendron* spp.
Poinsettia	*Euphorbia pulcherrima*
Privet	*Ligustrum* spp.
Rhododendron	*Rhododendron* spp.
Yam Bean	*Pachyrhizus erosus*

OUTDOOR PLANTS

American Yew	*Taxus canadensis*
Cowslip (*Marshmarigold)	*Caltha* spp.
Baneberry	*Actaea* spp.
Bittersweet Nightshade	*Solanum dulcamara*
Black Locust	*Robinia pseudoacacia*
Bloodroot	*Sanguinario* spp.
Blue-Green Algae (Some species toxic)	Schizophyceae spp.
Buckthorn	*Rhamnus* spp.
Buttercup	*Ranunculus* spp.

Calla Lilly	*Zantedeschia aethiopica*
Cherry Tree (bark, twigs, leaves & pits)	*Prunus* spp.
Christmas Candle	*Pedilanthus tithymaloides*
Clematis	*Clematis* spp.
Daphne	*Daphne* spp.
Death Camas	*Zygadenus elegans*
Deadly Amanita (mushroom)	*Amanita muscaria*
English Holly	*Ilex aquifolium*
Evergreen Trees (most can be dangerous)	Coniferal
English Yew	*Taxus baccata*
False Hellebore	*Veratrum woodii*
Foxglove (leaves & seeds)	*Digitalis purpurea*
Fly Agaric Mushrooms	*Amanita muscaria*
Golden Chain (*Laburnum)	*Laburnum anagyroides*
Henbane	*Hyocyanamus niger*
Hemlock	*Conium maculatum*
Honey Locust	*Gleditsia triacathos*
Horse Chestnut	*Aesculus* spp.
Indian Turnip	*Arisaema triphyllum*
Iris (*Blue Flag)	*Iris* spp.
Jack-In-The-Pulpit	*Aisaema triphyllum*
Jimsonweed (*Thornapple)	*Datura* spp.
Juniper	*Juniperus* spp.
Larkspur	*Delphinium* spp.
Locoweed	*Astragalus mollissimus*
Lords & Ladies (*Cuckoopint)	*Arum* spp.
Marijuana	*Cannabis sativa*
Mayapple	*Podophyllum* spp.
Mescal Bean	*Sophora* spp.
Mistletoe (berries)	*Santalales* spp. (Loranthaceae)
Mock Orange	*Poncirus* spp.
Monkshood	*Aconitum* spp.
Morning Glory	*Ipomoea* spp.
Mountain Laurel	*Kalmia latifolia*
Nutmeg	*Myristica fragrans*
Poison Ivy	*Toxicodendron radicans*
Poison Oak	*Toxicodendron quercifolium*
Pokeweed (*Inkberry)	*Phytolacca americans*
Potato (New Shoots)	*Solanum tuberosum*
Rhubarb (Leaves)	*Rheum rhaponticum*
Rosary Peas (*Indian Licorice)	*Abrus precatorius*
Skunk Cabbage	*Symplocarpus foetidus*

Snowdrop	*Galanthus nivalis*
Snow-On-The-Mountain (*Ghost-weed)	*Euphorbia marginata*
Snow Flake	*Leucojum vernum*
Sweet Pea	*Lathyrus latifolius*
Tobacco	*Nicotinia* spp.
Virginia Creeper	*Psedera quinquefolia*
Water Hemlock	*Cicuta maculata*
Western Yew	*Taxus breviflora*
Wisteria	*Wisteria* spp.

AIR POLLUTION

Birds are very sensitive to pollutants in the air. It is unwise to keep your bird in an area that is heavily polluted by cigarette or cigar smoke, gas and cooking fumes, or heavy dust in the air. Even the fumes given off by burning or overheated teflon pans, although not toxic to humans, can be toxic to birds.

These pollutants may cause chronic respiratory problems that are difficult if not impossible to clear up. I have known cases where birds constantly sneezed at home, but stopped without any treatment whatever when they were moved to the hospital environment.

If you are painting inside your house, move your birds elsewhere. Carbon monoxide, paint fumes, insecticide sprays, or even continual use of deodorizer sprays can be dangerous air pollutants for your bird. Similarly, insecticidal pest strips hanging in your bird room continuously may be "potentially" toxic to your birds. These strips give off poisonous vapours which kill insects and it is not recommended that birds be exposed to these vapours all the time. Toxicity will vary with the size of the room. Intermittent use is tolerated better, i.e. 3 days exposure, then 2 days unexposed, and repeat as needed.

OTHER PETS

The presence of dogs, cats or other large animals can be a potential danger to your bird. Instinct will drive your other pets to stalk or tease the newcomer. The larger birds are better able to defend themselves and gain the respect of a dog or cat. But small birds will likely be victimized.

If your other pets cannot be trained to leave their new "friend" alone, do not give them access to the bird. In the beginning, it is wise to expose your pets to one another for brief periods, while you keep a watchful eye over the proceedings. Do not leave them alone until you are confident the bird will be safe.

TELEVISION AND MUSIC

The sounds of music and television can be enjoyable to birds, providing

When properly introduced, your pets can enjoy each other's company.

they are exposed to it during their normal waking cycle. The low murmur of a radio is especially entertaining to the bird left by itself in the daytime. However, the crashing chords from a stereo turned up full can cause a bird as much distress as it does you. Use common sense regarding the volume of sound the bird is exposed to, and remember that your bird is a captive of whatever environment you choose to surround him with.

This same cautionary advice about sound levels also applies to your television set, with this additional warning. The cathodes of a colour television emit rays that could damage your bird's health in the long run. Rather than take the chance, do not place the bird's cage on top of, or too near, a colour set.

TOYS AND ENTERTAINMENT

Being alone, cooped up in a cage all day with nothing to do, is a very boring and frustrating experience. A lot of bird owners are away during the day, and this absence must be considered when setting up a bird's cage and environment. Birds may doze or rest a bit from time to time, but they really do not sleep much unless it is dark. In their waking hours, they need some form of entertainment.

Swings are a simple delight. They can be of many types: a wire frame with a wooden bottom, or a sagging loop of light rope, flexible rubber or plastic hose. Swings can be attached to the top or sides of the cage.

Climbing toys like ladders, rope and chains may be dangled down from a perch or the top of the cage. When using a chain, make sure that its links are

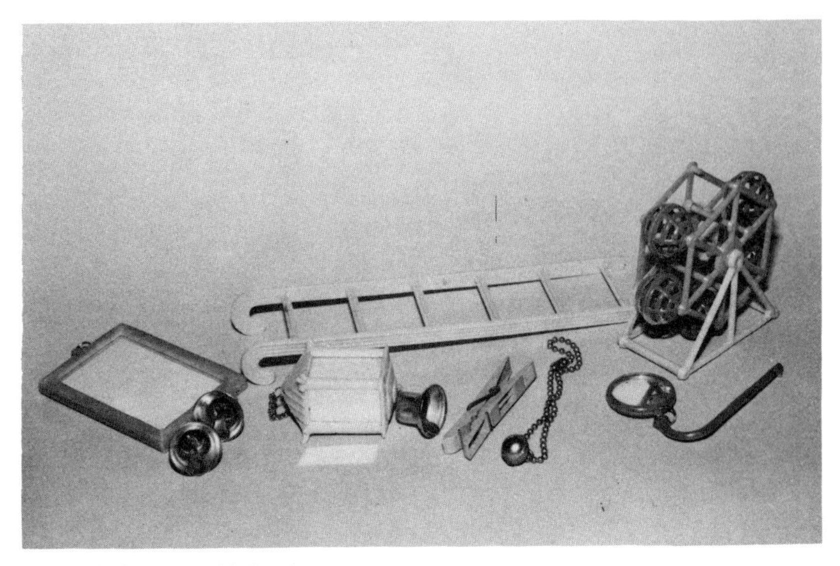

Toys help keep your bird active.

large enough that the bird's toes do not get caught.

Small bells seem to hold a special fascination for many birds who will often sit directly beneath them. Suspend the bell within easy reach of a favourite perch. If given to bigger birds, make sure the bell's clapper is attached firmly, so that the bird cannot chew it off and swallow it. The sound of little music box toys that play when the bird sits on the perch can also be quite entertaining.

Jangly, clanky items like keys suspended from a chain, little tin cups, or metal spoons are only a few of the common household items that can be adapted to amuse your bird.

Little plastic or wooden bobbing toys in the shape of birds and balls are often appreciated by some of the smaller species, such as budgies and cockatiels. These toys can be left on the floor of the cage, or attached to a perch.

Shiny objects like mirrors and metallic items are also highly appreciated. But watch that bigger birds do not break the mirror's glass and injure themselves, or chew up and fragment their plastic toys.

Having something to chew on has made many a bird happy. Wooden spools, little blocks of wood, pieces of fresh, bark-covered tree branch, small hard bones that will not fragment, cardboard boxes and rawhide chews; these things will help satisfy a natural chewing instinct in many species of birds, and keep them happy for hours[1]. Most of these items can be boiled periodically to clean and sterilize them. In general, the greater the chewability of a toy, the greater the pleasure it provides.

Birds love to hide in things.

Rubber toys, however, are a glaring exception to the rule. They can be very dangerous. Once eaten, rubber is acted upon by the digestive enzymes, which release toxins that deteriorate the bowel lining and paralyse the intestinal muscles. The result can be blockage of the bowel and death, so make a point of keeping rubber toys away from your pet.

Birds love to hide in things. A privacy box, a small, hollow cardboard tube, or even a simple paper bag lying open on the cage floor gives your bird a whole new world to explore.

Large birds will also enjoy playing with coconut shells, sea shells, orange peels, dried gourds and banana skins, or raw vegetables like carrots and potatoes.

Now that you realize the endless variety of toys available, try not to clutter the cage or make it so crowded that your bird cannot move about freely. You should have a variety of toys on hand, but restrain yourself from putting all of them in the cage at once. Rotating them is best, and then your bird will get the maximum pleasure out of his different playthings.

Birds may be frightened of new toys at first, but have patience. In a few days, they will probably accept the new things and begin to play with them.

---

1. Birds also find paper chewing quite entertaining, although they rarely eat the paper itself. If the paper is actually consumed it could be the indication of a depraved appetite, which is a medical problem that requires discussion with your veterinarian.

Bathing makes a bird feel good about itself.

BATHING

Most birds like their bath immensely, and they all need it. Bathing is required to keep the feathers clean, and it encourages preening or grooming of the feathers. Some birds like to splash around in a dish of water, some like to be "rained" on, and some timid sorts prefer to nestle in wet grass or greens.

For those that like to splash in water, a shallow dish or pan will serve, or a commercial bird bath can be attached to the cage. Your bird may even take a liking to the kitchen sink, providing the water is shallow enough.

For those that prefer to be rained on, such as the larger parrot types, you can sprinkle water on them, take them in the shower with you, or mist them with a plant sprayer. A gentle rather than heavy spray is best. A few of these birds also like to wet themselves by walking back and forth under a gently running tap.

Some parrakeets[2] enjoy wetting themselves on damp vegetation like carrot tops, while budgies often prefer to roll in wet greens or grass on the bottom of the cage. A 12–15 cm (4½–6in.) square piece of grass sod with the grass 5–7 cm (2–2½ in.) tall is ideal for this purpose. The grass is also a handy source of greens for your bird[3].

A little experimentation on your part will determine how your bird prefers his bath. Frequency of bathing varies with the bird: many like daily and others occasional baths. Your bird should be given the opportunity to bathe at least once or twice a week. A morning bath is advisable, giving the bird an opportunity to dry out during the day, because household temperatures often drop at night, and a damp bird might chill and become sick. Do

---

2. Many Americans commonly refer to the budgie as "parrakeet"; however, the term parrakeet delineates a particular species and is so used in this text.

3. Leave it in the cage for an hour or two, twice a week. The grass sod can be grown in a flat dish or pot of some sort, providing allowance is made for drainage.

make sure that your bird has a warm, draught-free place where he can dry out and preen his feathers.

FLYING FREE

Birds released from their cages to fly free in the house will benefit both physically and mentally from the experience. They are often seen at their best on these occasions.

Yet at the same time, a free-flying bird can wing his way into countless perils. You will never know what a jungle your home is until you release an innocent bird into its depths. He can fall victim to the most bizarre happenings, disappearing up a vacuum, for instance, or plummeting into a toilet bowl. Curiosity might drop him into the family stew pot, or land him square between the cat's delighted paws. Bizarre; but accidents like these have happened. If they sound comic in the retelling, many were tragic when they occurred.

Before letting your bird free, close the doors to dangerous territories like the kitchen, bathroom, and, of course, the outdoors. Once he is free, be conscious of the bird's whereabouts. Through experience you will learn to anticipate your bird's movements – the places and things he likes to explore – and know what must be done to secure these areas for his safety. If proper care is taken, both you and your bird can enjoy his freedom.

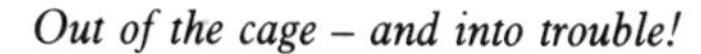

Out of the cage – and into trouble!

LIGHT AND SLEEP

The metabolism and function of a bird are largely controlled by the amount of light and darkness it is exposed to over a 24 hour period. Summertime provides more hours of light than wintertime does, and most birds synchronize their waking cycle to the amount of natural daylight they experience. In nature, birds go to sleep when it gets dark and wake up when it gets light. Similarly, cage birds should not be kept awake for long hours after nightfall, but rather should be covered with a heavy cloth that shuts out the light and some noise. The cloth cover will be removed the following morning.

Even though your bird may want to visit with you and "stay up", it should still be put to bed at dark. Exceptions can occasionally be made if you have been away all day, leaving the bird alone. Under these circumstances, it would appreciate an hour or two of your time before going to bed. Birds need 9 to 12 hours of sleep each night, and if they are deprived of this rest, they often become sick or neurotic.

Don't Be Alarmed – It's Normal

You may have noticed your bird yawning. Don't worry about it – birds often yawn, just as mammals do.

Birds may stand or sleep with one leg tucked up next to their body. This one-legged stance should not be confused with lameness.

They may also snooze periodically during the day, or awaken during the night to have a snack.

On occasion, sleeping birds will startle awake, and then flap about the cage for a short period. Like people, they do not always sleep soundly through the night.

ARTIFICIAL LIGHT

When birds are exposed to a lot of artificial light and little or no sunlight, they do not benefit from the essential rays that are necessary for good health. Your birds, whether you have one, two or many, will stay healthier if the form of artificial light you use is the Vita-Lite® fluorescent bulb[4], which comes in various lengths. The light rays from these bulbs are very close to daylight. They are available in plant nurseries, major department and hardware stores, and some pet shops.

---

4. Manufactured by Duro-Test Electric, Ltd., Downsview, Ontario.

3
Tips on Care

HOW TO HOLD YOUR BIRD

Anyone who handles birds, whether for beak and nail trims or for examination and treatment, should understand how to restrain them properly. Proper restraint will not only minimize potential injury to the bird, but will also protect the handler. Some of the medium to large-sized birds can do substantial damage with their beaks. Even a small bird's bite can be painful, especially from the psittacine species.

A word of caution: the jaws of large birds such as macaws have the power to amputate a finger, or at the very least to remove a large piece of flesh. Always treat their beaks with a good deal of respect.

When handling birds, it is important to know that they do not have a diaphragm as mammals do; their breathing is totally dependent on the expansion and contraction of their chest wall. Therefore, the handler must not constrict this chest movement or the result will be death by suffocation. The bird should be held gently, but firmly enough to prevent escape and allow the procedure required.

Small birds can be secured in the following manner. Hold a paper towel or small cloth open in your hand, catching part of it between your first two fingers. Approach the bird slowly in order not to frighten it, then grasp it firmly in your towelled hand and remove it from the cage. A helpful suggestion: you may find that excitable birds are caught more easily in the

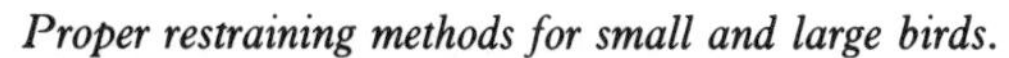

Proper restraining methods for small and large birds.

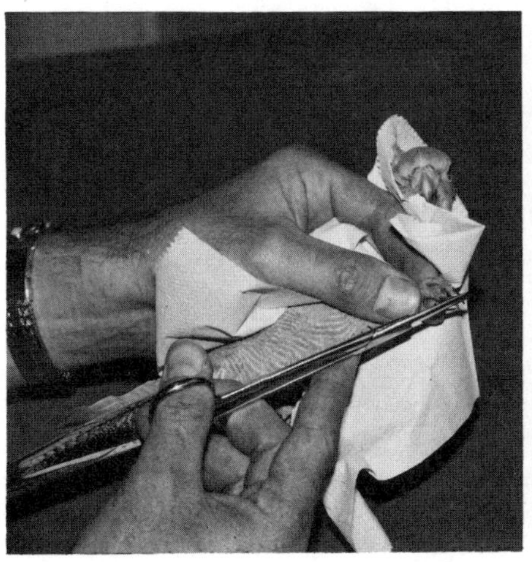

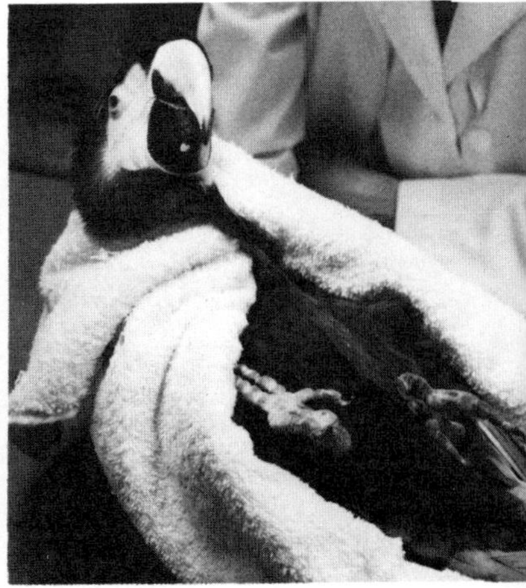

dark. First take note of where the bird is in its cage, then have someone turn out the light, and grasp the bird as described above. Turn the light on again and continue with your procedure.

Once the bird is in hand, arrange your towel so that it is between your fingers and the bird's head. When he bites, it will be the paper and not you. Hold the bird's paper-wrapped head and neck between your first two fingers, and let the body of the bird lie in the palm of your hand, holding it still with your thumb and other fingers. Now it is an easy matter to hold the bird's leg between your thumb and third finger, and either cut the nails, or treat the foot as needed.

Small birds can be manipulated into any position that is required for examination or treatment just by varying this basic hold. The paper or cloth may not even be necessary with the smaller birds whose bite is less painful, such as canaries, finches and similar species.

The larger psittacine birds should be handled a little differently. They can be caught from behind by placing a thick towel over their head and body. Scoop them up and grasp the neck from the rear, firmly encircling it (outside the towel) with your fingers. The towel is folded around the bird's body and meets at the front, thus to prevent the wings from flapping and getting injured. Uncover the head once the bird is wrapped properly. One person should hold the bird, while another examines and treats it. The towel edges, which are in front of the bird, separate easily, giving you access to the feet, legs and body. The bird usually clutches the towel with one foot while you are working on the other.

When you are examining the head and beak, hold the upper and lower parts of the beak together with one hand while you work with the other. Be careful not to injure the tongue, which the bird often tries to stick out between its beak.

Ducks, geese and poultry can be restrained by grasping the base of the wings together, which spreads them out and over the back. This prevents the bird's inclination to flap its wings vigorously. Another person is then able to hold whatever part of the body needs to be worked on.

Birds of prey such as hawks and owls can be held in the same manner as ducks and geese; however, their legs and feet must also be held together because of their dangerous talons. You may also find it prudent to restrain the head, which has a very sharp beak.

There are several parts of the bird's body, specifically his toenails, beak, feathers and wings, which need your close attention. In fact, learning how to care properly for these vital parts will enable you to interpret the bird's state of health from different signs like the length of his beak or the condition of his feathers.

Observing your bird daily familiarizes you with the norms in his growth and activities. As a result, you can be critical of any deviation that occurs and will be able to specify these changes to your veterinarian, if necessary.

TOENAILS

Everyone knows that their own fingernails and toenails grow at a regular rate, and must be trimmed frequently. The same applies to birds. In wild birds, nail growth and nail wear balance naturally. But the nails of caged birds are seldom exposed to the same abrasive wear as their wild counterparts. Consequently, the nails grow excessively long, unless you keep them trimmed properly. Long nails make it difficult for the bird to perch or climb, and the nails can get caught on various things and cause injury.

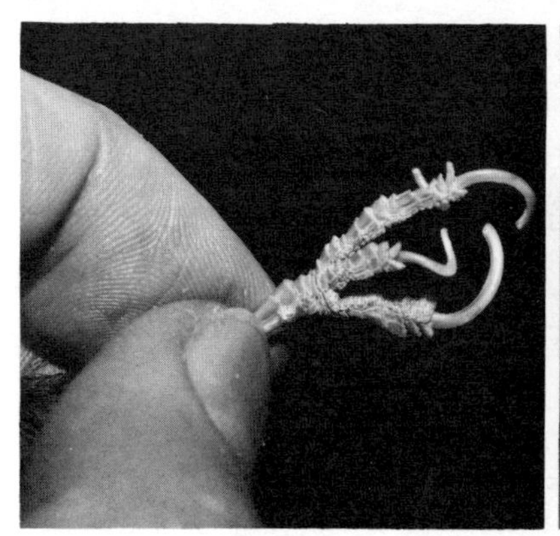

Unless properly trimmed, long nails can cause injury.

When trimming the nails, it is best to pare off a little at a time, so that you do not cut into and expose the nail's quick. The "quick" refers to the blood and nerve supply that grows partway down the nail. In light-coloured nails the quick is easily seen, but black nails hide it completely. If the quick is cut, the nail will bleed profusely and cause the bird pain.

This bleeding must be stopped immediately because birds cannot tolerate the loss of much blood. Apply a moistened styptic pencil, silver nitrate, iron subsulfate or a liquid anticoagulant to the bleeding area[1]. Then take a dry piece of cotton and apply a little pressure to the nail until all bleeding stops. Sometimes heat cautery is needed to stop really stubborn bleeding. Heat a small metal object like a pocket knife to a red glow and touch it carefully to the bleeding area, which will sear it.

If the bird has lost any appreciable amount of blood, it should be kept warm 26–29°C (80–85°F), and the cage should be covered for a few hours to keep the bird quiet. This will help it get over the shock of blood loss, and lessen the chance of renewed bleeding.

---

1. Such as HematrolTM, a product manufactured by Burns-Biotec Laboratories Division, Chromalloy Pharmaceutical, Inc., Oakland, California or QuickstopTM powder made by Arc Laboratories, P.O. Box 18884, Irvine, California, 92713 USA.

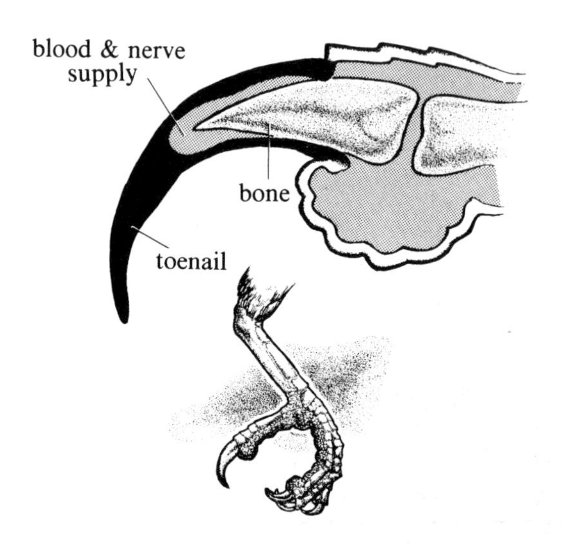

It takes good judgment and practice to be able to cut nails properly, and it is not advisable for the novice to attempt it. Take your bird to your veterinarian for regular health checkups, and the nails can be trimmed at the same time.

BEAK

A bird's beak is a multi-purpose instrument that is absolutely essential to the bird's survival. It is used for such diverse purposes as nest building, grooming and preening the feathers, feeding the young, grasping, breaking or tearing apart food, climbing, self-defence and communication.

An abnormally long beak will interfere with the bird's eating.

The beak consists of a hard keratinized or horn-like covering over the jaws of the bird, and it grows continually. All the activities mentioned above help wear the beak down, as does direct rubbing on hard materials like perches, cuttlebone and mineral blocks. The rubbing of lower beak against upper beak also helps maintain its proper shape and length. In spite of this, some birds cannot wear the beak enough and it grows far too long. This abnormal length will interfere with eating, and in psittacine birds, like budgies and parrots, the extended beak may even curve under and protrude into the bird's neck.

Keep an eye on the length of your bird's beak, something that will also be checked during routine visits to your veterinarian.

The rate of growth for the upper beak of certain birds has been suggested as: 3.4–3.8 cm (1⅓–1½ in.) per year in the canary; 7.5 cm (3 in.) per year in the budgie, and 3.2 cm (1¼ in.) per year for the parrot. Note that the lower beak grows at a slightly lesser rate[2].

Anyone who trims beaks and nails should learn the proper methods of catching and restraining the bird in order to minimize fright and injury. But, as mentioned in the section on toenails, it is ill-advised for the novice to attempt the delicate task of trimming.

Beaks can split, break or crack in the process if great care is not taken. The beak must be trimmed exactly to its normal shape and length; cut it too short and the beak will bleed profusely. As with the toenails, there is a nerve and blood supply in the beak, and it extends much farther into the length of the beak than the quick does in the toenails. In short, it is best to leave the task to an experienced person like your veterinarian.

Birds should be given lots of opportunities to use their beaks and wear them down naturally. The entire parrot family should be offered chew sticks, tree branches, pieces of wood, nuts, and bones to chew on. Incidentally, these materials will not only help wear down the beak, but will also provide entertainment for your bird.

Busy birds seldom have problems with abnormal beak length. Conversely, overgrown beaks may be the sign of a less active bird, and a reduction in its activity could mean the bird is gradually getting sick. In the early stages of illness, birds often show no visible symptoms; the signs may be quite subtle. Be an observant owner and do not take your bird's health for granted. Watch him closely each day, and learn to interpret how he is from how he looks and what he does.

FEATHER CARE

Feathers are fairly delicate structures, and they are essential to the bird's

---

2. T.J. Lafeber, D.V.M. *Tender Loving Care For Pet Birds*, p. 56.

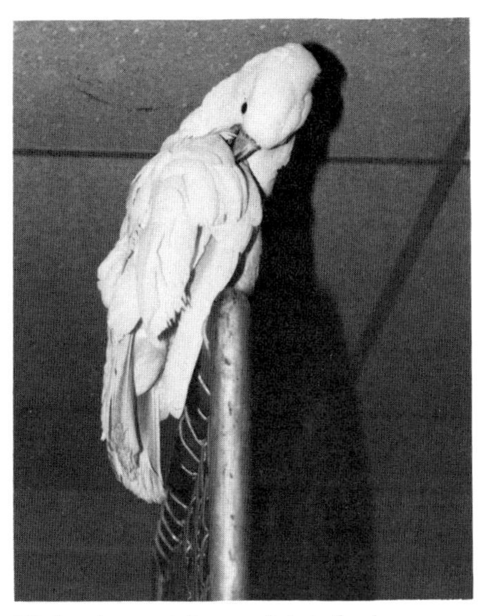

Birds take special care of their feathers.

being. They help to preserve and maintain body heat; they also repel water and add buoyancy to water birds. They give a bird his colour, his ability to fly, and they protect his skin from the sun and other hazards.

Birds will preen or groom their feathers with their beaks, taking great care to keep them in neat, orderly condition. Frequent baths will help keep the feathers clean and stimulate the bird to groom them as he dries out. Only the bird can groom his feathers properly, but you, his owner, can help him greatly by ensuring that certain conditions are met. Provide him with suitable bathing facilities and a clean cage that is big enough, with sufficient perch clearance, that feathers are not damaged by rubbing or fouled by excreta. And remember, a nutritious, well-balanced diet is the basis of good healthy feathers.

FEATHER-DUSTING

You may have noticed how much wild birds and game fowl (including domestic types) enjoy a dust bath. They will find an area to their liking and flap around or rub in it, working the dust into their feathers. They usually seek a patch of fine abrasive sand, which when rubbed into the feathers sinks deep into the fluff where dead air space has formed, and also works its way between the contour feathers that overlap each other. As the sand penetrates these areas, it polishes away at the cupped and frayed edges of the feathers, and removes the ragged portions that have not fallen away through normal wear. This all helps to maintain healthier, stronger, more efficient feathers. Feather-dusting is a natural and necessary activity for birds, and is in no way related to the presence of external parasites. Wild birds and game birds should be provided with a container of very fine sand dust to help keep their feathers healthy.

OIL AND FEATHERS DO NOT MIX

A discussion of feathers would be incomplete without a few cautionary words on the use of oily and greasy products.

I have seen many cases where a bird owner, through his own good intentions or some very bad advice, has applied oil or petroleum jelly to an "itchy" bird. Most of these birds become seriously ill and are beyond help by the time they reach an animal hospital. Their deaths are needless.

Oil and feathers do not mix, and this rule extends to all greasy products. Keep them away from your bird. When these products are rubbed into the skin area, they tend to spread out and oil all the surrounding feathers. If enough is used, the major part of the bird's feathers will become stuck together, and the bird will go frantic trying to groom out the offensive material. As a result of this slicked-down, sticky mess, the feathers lose their insulating or heat-conserving ability, and the bird becomes chilled, sick and often dies.

One of the most commonly used products on the market today is petroleum jelly. Any ointment that contains this product should never be applied to a bird. In fact, do not apply any form of grease and oil to the bird's skin, legs or feet.

On occasion a bird flying about the kitchen has accidentally fallen into a pan of oil or grease. Do be careful that such products are out of the way before the bird is given his freedom.

If a bird does somehow get oil on its feathers, the oil must be removed quickly and the environmental temperature raised to between 26–29°C (80–85°F) to maintain the bird's body heat.

To remove the feather contamination, wash the bird gently with warm water and a mild soap like baby shampoo[3]. The soaping and rinsing may have to be repeated several times to remove all the oil and grease. During the final rinse, make sure all the soap is removed. Gently dry the excess water with a soft towel or some facial tissue, and then blow dry with a hair dryer. The bird should be kept in a warm environment for a few days after this experience to minimize the shock of the whole process.

An oil-covered bird rapidly loses its body heat.

3. Environmentalists who treat bird oil-slick victims in contaminated areas also recommend Lux Liquid AmberTM detergent, manufactured by Lever Detergents Ltd., Toronto, Ontario.

MOULTING

Birds change their feather covering at regular intervals, and this cycle is called moulting. The old, damaged feathers are dropped and new ones grow in their place. Feathers are lost by being picked or shaken out as they loosen in the follicles.

Some birds moult twice in a year, but the majority change their feathers only once a year. Moulting generally occurs in the spring after the normal reproduction period. It can also be continuous throughout the year with the heaviest moult occurring in the spring and early summer, as is the case with most members of the parrot family. Canaries and other passerine birds moult gradually over several months from May to December. Immature birds will also change their plumage when they become sexually mature.

Most birds only shed a few feathers at a time from certain areas of the body, and so retain their ability to fly and keep warm. However, some water fowl do lose all their wing feathers at once and are actually incapable of flight for a short period.

As soon as an old feather is lost, a new one will begin to grow immediately, providing that the old shaft has been removed from the feather follicle. It takes about six weeks for a new feather to grow in. Called pin or blood feathers, these new feathers grow out as spiky shafts that will eventually lose their sheath-like covering. The inner feathers emerge, and then fluff out and expand to their normal shape. The sheath covering is picked off by the bird and its broken pieces fall in dandruff-like particles, which may be grey, white or black in colour. Birds constantly preen the new feathers to remove this outer sheath, and their owners often grow anxious, believing that the bird is picking at itself because it has "bugs". In fact, the bird's behaviour is quite normal.

While it grows, the pin feather is dark, both at the base and partway up the shaft, because of the blood supply it contains. It will bleed profusely if damaged. In such a case, pluck out the bleeding feather, and then apply a piece of dry cotton and light pressure to the wound until the bleeding stops.

When their birds are moulting, many people have observed that the new feathers appear powdery. Indeed, this substance is called "powder down"; it is produced by the new feathers themselves and especially by the downy under-feathers. Powder down, combined with secretions from the oil glands, help to lubricate the feathers and reduce feather wear.

As you can appreciate, moulting is a very stressful time for the bird. Most song birds stop singing during moulting, and start again when all the feathers have regrown. It uses a lot of body resources to grow new feathers and this drain can leave the bird susceptible to disease. As always, proper nutrition is essential because good food will lessen the physical strain on your bird. There are commercial "moulting foods" on the market, but these are simply variety seed mixes that contain better nutrition. Assuming that you already feed him a carefully selected seed mix, some cooked egg yolk given daily will provide your bird with the extra protein he needs during moulting.

Warmth is as necessary to a moulting bird as proper rest and sleep. A bird is more vulnerable to chilling and sickness during a moult than at any other time because of his lowered body resistance. You can help by keeping him warm, quiet, and covering his cage for longer periods.

Don't Be Alarmed – It's Normal

Birds have very thin skin. Occasionally, seeds in the crop may become visible through the skin because of moulting, feather loss, or a separation between the feathers that usually cover the crop area. These seeds may be visible at the sides of the neck as well, and are nothing to worry about.

CLIPPING WINGS

There are many ways to clip a bird's wings. If a bird is to be permanently grounded, as in the case of semi-wild waterfowl like ducks, geese or swans, the end of each wing is surgically removed in a procedure called "pinioning". Birds treated in this manner will never fly properly again. It is not an advisable procedure for pet cage birds.

The usual way to prevent cage birds from flying is to clip the feathers on one wing. There are many different ways of doing this and opinions vary greatly as to which way works the best.

I use the following method. The secondary flight feathers, except for those three or four nearest the body and one or two of the primary feathers at the wing tip are cut even with, or a little shorter than the tertiary feathers on one wing. The two feathers left at the tip of the wing maintain the balanced appearance of the crossed wing tips when they are folded over the rump of the bird. Similarly, once the wing is folded, the four unclipped feathers close to the body hide the cut edge.

Cutting only one wing puts the bird off balance, so that it cannot gain altitude when it attempts to fly. Some birds will require a few of the primary wing feathers removed from the opposite wing as well. This will keep the bird from flying until the cut feathers are shed during the next moult. If flight is to be controlled longer, the new feathers must be cut again, as described above. The occasional bird that can still fly after this method has been used, may also require the additional clipping of one or two end primary feathers.

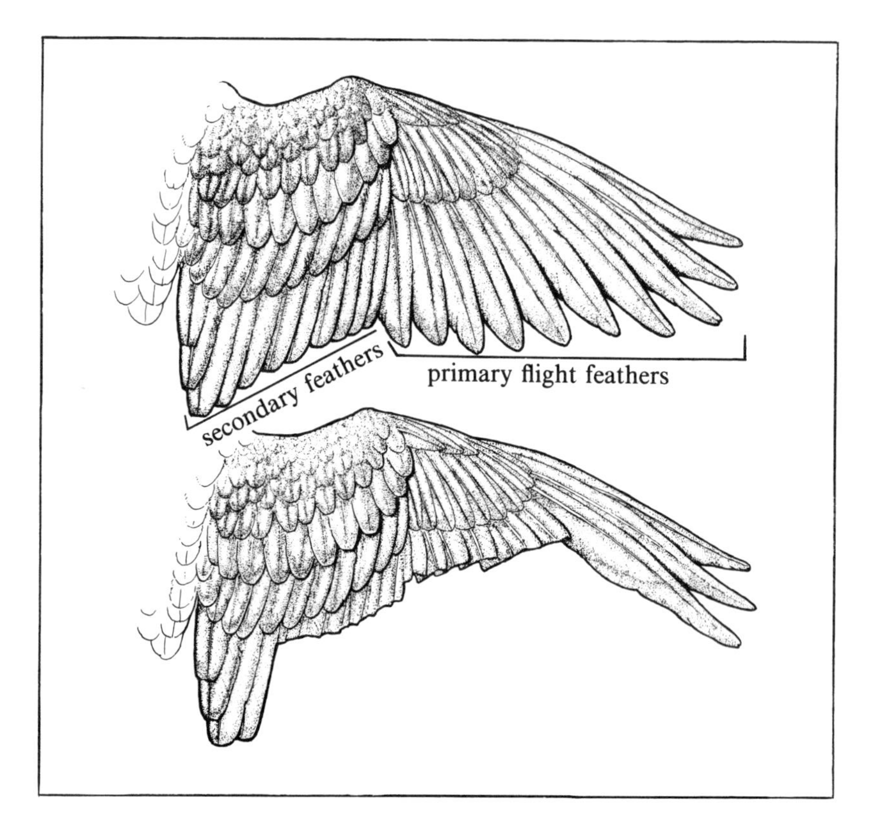

A spread wing (dorsal or top view), before and after being clipped.

If flight is to be controlled for a short period, these same feathers can be plucked out (which is painful to the bird), and the bird will be grounded for the six to eight weeks it take for these feathers to regrow.

LEG CHAINS

Some bird owners, especially the owners of larger birds, rely on leg chains rather than wing clipping to control their pet's flight. These owners enjoy seeing their bird out in the open, but because the bird has not been trained to return, they cannot risk free-flying it. To prevent the bird's escape, they fasten a clamp around the bird's leg with a screw device, and then attach a short piece of light chain to the clamp. This, they feel, will keep their pet safe and sound.

True, the bird will not escape unless the chain is dropped. But the bird itself is far from being safe and sound. If something happens to startle the bird, as is quite possible in an outdoor situation, the bird can panic, take flight and in seconds be at the end of its chain, which has such stopping force that the bird's leg snaps and fractures badly. Leg fractures in the large psittacine birds are very difficult to repair because of the bird's resistance to splints and casts.

In my opinion, leg chains are very dangerous and should not be used. Instead, I recommend having the wing feathers clipped, so that the bird cannot fly.

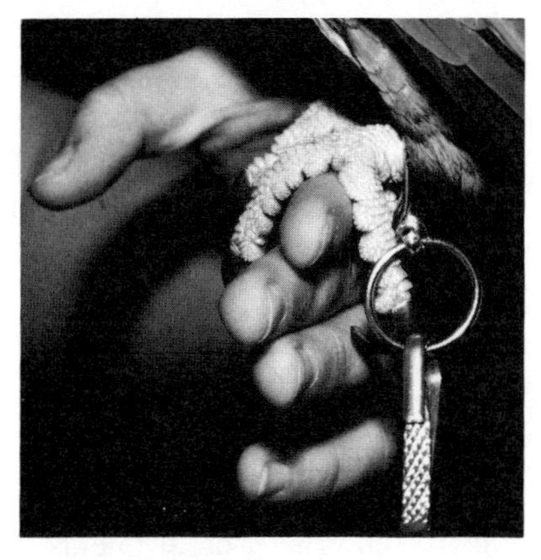

Leg chains are dangerous and should not be used.

INTRODUCING NEW BIRDS

As you know, your new bird is identified by the aluminium leg band that records its year of birth. Take note of this date, and then have the band removed by either a competent pet shop owner, or your veterinarian. If the band remains on your bird, it can only lead to complications, snagging on things, trapping dead skin and debris, and ultimately exerting enough pressure to effectively cut off the blood circulation to the bird's foot. As the condition grows worse, swelling, death of the foot, and gangrene cause the bird great suffering. Think of the birds whose legs have actually had to be amputated in the end, and you will make haste to get that leg band removed.

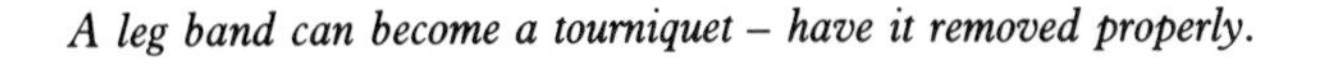

A leg band can become a tourniquet – have it removed properly.

If you already have one or more birds, and are about to introduce yet another, you should observe the following:

Quarantine – isolate the new bird for at least 30 days to make sure it is not carrying some disease that your other birds might catch. I have seen many disastrous problems arise from not observing this rule.

Check-up – have the new bird examined by your veterinarian. And remember, even though the bird appears healthy, it may still be incubating a disease. A quarantine period should still be observed.

Compatibility – if the new bird is to be housed with others, make sure they will not bully, harm or kill one another. After the quarantine period, put the birds' cages side by side for a few days before actually mingling them, so that the new bird can be gradually accepted.

Small birds – beware of caging a small bird with a large bird that might injure or kill it. Even the small bird flying about innocently and landing on a large bird's cage could end up with a badly mangled or amputated leg because of a hostile bite through the cage bars.

OUTDOOR HAZARDS

In the summertime, many people move their pets outside, putting their birds in outdoor aviaries, suspending the bird's cage from a tree, or simply leaving the bird on an outside perch. The fresh air and stimulating environment will certainly do the bird good, but do be careful to take the necessary precautions for the bird's safety and well-being. For instance, even if his wings are clipped, a bird on an outside perch is sorely tempted to investigate his surroundings. He will also be subject to dangers from wild birds (their droppings can carry diseases), dogs, cats and predatory birds that look on him as crow bait. Do not leave him unattended. As well, be sure he has some shelter to which he can retreat when the sun grows too warm, or he grows weary of things and wants a little privacy.

Birds enjoy being outdoors, but make sure they are adequately protected.

You should also be careful about the kind of food your bird is exposed to. There is a type of bacteria called clostridium botulinum that grows in decomposed organic material and rotten food; it produces a very potent toxin. Unless outdoor aviaries and cages are cleaned regularly, the bird is apt to consume some bad food and fall victim to botulism. The bird's consumption of this toxin will result in death.

TRANSPORTING BIRDS

At one time or another, most bird owners are faced with the problem of having to transport their pet. Whether it is a short trip to the veterinarian, a move to a new house or apartment, or a journey of several hundred miles, a little planning and extra care will keep your bird safe and healthy.

The four most important things to consider when transporting a bird are:

Environment – birds are quite sensitive to sudden changes in temperature. Placing a bird in an environment that is hotter or colder than what it is accustomed to can be very dangerous.

Security – make sure the bird's cage or shipping container is firmly secured to prevent any movement or shifting, whether on your car seat or within a more spacious compartment.

Quiet – birds become agitated very easily. A small transport cage will limit the bird's movement and the potential for harming itself. You may also consider a light cover over the cage, so that the bird will be shielded from the abrupt changes that accompany most moves.

Documentation – a bill of sale for the bird will be helpful. In Canada, health certificates are only good for a maximum of ten days before they must be renewed. If you are travelling to another country, check well in advance with its authorities for the proper import or export papers required, and arrange for quarantine of the bird if necessary. Canadian officials are: Animal Contagious Diseases Dept., Agriculture Canada, Ottawa, Ontario. For USA information and regulations, contact: Import–Export Staff, Veterinary Services, APHIS, US Department of Agriculture, Hyattsville, Maryland, 20782, USA.

For import and export information in other countries, apply to:

UNITED KINGDOM: Ministry of Agriculture, Fisheries & Food, Import/ Export Section, Hook Rise South, Tolworth, Surbiton, Surrey KI6 7NF, or Department of The Environment, Wildlife Conservation Licensing Section, Tollgate House, Houlton Street, Bristol. BS2 9DJ.

NETHERLANDS: Ministerie van Cultur, Recreatie en Maatschappelijk Werk, Directie Naut-en Landschapsbescherming 10, Postbus 5406, 2280 HK Rijswijk.

GERMANY: Bundesministerium fur Ernahrung, Landwirtschaft und Forsten, Referat 623, Postfach 140270, D–5300 Bonn 1, Germany.

Short distance moves present few problems. In warm weather, if you are moving your bird by car, open the window nearest its cage about half an inch, for a supply of fresh air, and keep the bird out of direct sunlight. In cool weather, wrap your bird's cage in a blanket, and warm up the car beforehand. On longer car trips, stop every 3 to 4 hours to give the bird a half-hour's break during which it can eat, drink and rest.

Long distance moves can be very hard on your bird if you do not plan them carefully. If you are travelling with the bird, keep it in a pet carrier under your seat. If you are shipping your bird by plane, bus or train, make sure it is being transported in an area that is heated and properly ventilated. Have your pet shipped on a direct route, as delays and transfers only cause additional problems, and record the number of your shipping receipt. You should also arrange to have someone waiting to collect the bird when it arrives.

Before you ship your bird, call the airline or bus company and ask for the official in charge of shipping live cargo. He or she will be able to help you select the best route and safest method of transporting your pet.

ESTIMATING THE AGES OF BIRDS

Unless the history of a bird is known exactly, such as when it was born, or it is wearing a leg band that has the year of birth, it is very difficult to assess the exact age of that bird. Birds do not have distinctive changes that occur at specific ages except when they are very young. A very old bird can be assessed as very old, but ageing it exactly is impossible. Some of the psittacine species do acquire a scurfy or scaly appearance to their feet and legs at four to five years of age, but other than this it is sheer guess work. An old bird may have some feather loss to varying degrees at the edge of the skin junction with the beak. Immature birds in many species do have some feather colour differences which have usually disappeared by the time they are a year of age, and some species may show a difference in the eye colour.

SEXING BIRDS

As more and more people are becoming interested in breeding birds, it is absolutely necessary that they know the sex of the birds they are trying to breed. Many species of birds are not dimorphic in their featheration, which means basically that the sexes look alike. It only stands to reason that if you put two birds of known opposite sex together in a breeding environment, that your chances of them breeding and raising young are tremendously greater than just putting two birds of unknown sex together.

Several methods of determining sex have been tried, from plasma steroid assay[1], cytology[2], or counting cell chromosomes and faecal steroid analysis[3], to direct laparoscopy where the gonads are viewed directly via a surgical operation using an endoscope which allows direct visualization of the ovaries or testicles through a small instrument with a light source that is inserted into the abdominal cavity.

The laparoscopic method has proven to be the most reliable technique and should only be done under sterile technique by an experienced veterinarian. This method not only allows the doctor to determine the sex of the bird, but also to assess the stage of sexual activity of the bird by seeing the size of the ovary or testicles.

---

1. Dieter, M.P., "Sex determination of eagles, owls and herons by analysing plasma steroid hormones", Spec. scient. Rep. U.S. Fish & Wildlife Service No. 167.

2. Mengden, G.A. and Stock, A.D., "A preliminary report on the application of current cytological techniques to sexing birds", *Int. Zoo Yb.* 16:138–141 1976.

3. Czekala, N.M. and Lasley, B.L., "A technical note on sex determination in monomorphic birds using faecal steroid analysis", *Int. Zoo Yb.* 17:209–211, 1977.

4
Feeding Your Bird

ESTABLISH A ROUTINE

Like people and animals, birds derive a sense of security from day to day routine. By presenting food and water, or performing activities like the cleaning of its cage in the same, consistent manner, you quickly teach a bird what to expect and when to expect it. Even more than people and animals, birds are shocked by a break in routine. They are suspicious of change, it frightens them, and their food and water consumption may temporarily drop.

It is best to feed your bird a little in the morning and a little at night. In this way, the bird is usually hungry when you feed it and will eat most of what you offer. You run little risk of developing a fussy eater with this method.

Most bird owners are in the habit of leaving the seed dish in the cage and filling it continuously. This is ill-advised. Give only enough seed, morning and night, so that all the previous seed will have been eaten by the time you give the next feeding. If there is still some left, cut down a bit on the amount you give. Of course his daily ration of fruit, vegetables and greens will remain in the bird's cage all day, so that he always has other foodstuffs to peck away at. The idea of regulating his seed intake is to establish a healthy

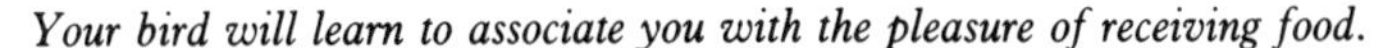
Your bird will learn to associate you with the pleasure of receiving food.

balance, where the bird is eating just enough; he should not be spending several hungry hours before receiving his next seed portion. A little trial and error will soon determine the right amount to give him.

Wild birds eat primarily in the morning and late afternoon or evening. Cage birds do much better if they are kept to this same schedule. Your bird may act as though he is starving to death when you first change over to this routine, but he will adjust to it and thrive.

Regulated feeding is often used as a means to tame birds. A bird that is slightly hungry will come to you for food, and soon learn to associate you with the pleasure of receiving it. If he is a little hungry, you can teach your bird to sit on your hand and eat from your fingers. An overfed bird is much less responsive to this training method.

Owners should observe exactly what their birds are consuming each day. Both the amount and the variety should be noted, so that you are familiar with the bird's normal eating pattern. Any deviation from this norm could indicate a sick bird.

PROPER DIET

The major cause of common disease problems in pet birds is an improper diet, which leads to malnutrition, dietary deficiencies and often death. A balanced diet must be provided if the bird is to be kept alive and healthy.

Because of their small size, high metabolic rate (the speed of chemical changes within the body) and short digestive tract, birds require a large volume of food to meet their needs.

"Fussy eaters" are usually malnourished birds because they will not eat a proper diet. These birds are listless; they do not talk, sing or fill out properly. They moult frequently, their feathers are poor, and life is shortened by their vulnerability to sickness and disease. Ironically, some malnourished birds can even be obese. You can create such a bird by continually feeding it a poor seed mixture that contains insufficient variety.

SEEDS

The only way to achieve good nutrition is to feed your bird a variety of foodstuffs. A good seed mixture is the basic ingredient in your bird's total diet needs. In selecting this mixture, look carefully at its contents and read the label critically. Buy only quality products that have a sufficient variety of seeds in them, rather than simply trusting to the discretion of a brandname manufacturer. It is better to purchase a quality mixture from a pet shop that knows birds and mixes their own fresh seed, than to buy some of the boxed commercial mixtures that are of poorer quality. Use commercial boxed seed only when the fresh is not available.

Treat foods, moulting food, song food and conditioner food are called

Treat and conditioner foods are available at pet shops.

supplemental seeds, and are basically a different variety of seed types, some of which have a vitamin-mineral supplementation[1]. These should be fed in a treat cup 2 or 3 times a week on a regular basis, and daily during the moulting period.

Do not let your bird get in the habit of eating only one or two varieties of seed, or you will end up with a malnourished bird. If your bird is this kind of an eater, let his hunger build up a little, and then provide a good variety mixed with a minimal amount of his favourite seed. You can also help him by continually removing the top layer of seed husks in his dish. Your bird may not be digging down through these husks to reach the whole seeds below.

Be sparing with millet sprays or honey stick seed clusters, and do not leave them in the cage all the time. Birds love these titbits; they eat them like candy and tend to leave their other seeds uneaten. A "candy" offering once a week is enough. Even half a stick per week will suffice for small birds like finches, canaries, budgies and cockatiels.

The seed you buy should be fresh, and, if so, will offer the maximum in nutritional value to your bird. Make sure you preserve this quality by keeping the seed clean and free of foreign matter like dust and rodent droppings.

Mouldy seed should not be fed to your bird. Mould growing in seed has a web-like appearance, and it can produce harmful toxins. These toxins could kill the birds that consume them.

Sometimes little beetles and their hairy larvae are found in the seed. This may be alarming to you, but it is not harmful to the bird. Remember that a lot of birds eat insects. You can kill any insects by heating the seed in the oven on a flat tray at 82°C (180°F) for half an hour. Do not go over 100°C (212°F) or you will destroy some of the nutritional value of the seeds[2].

FRUIT, VEGETABLES AND GREENS

Some form of fruit, vegetables or leafy greens should be fed to your bird every day. Some of either, or a piece of each, can be left in the cage with the

---

1. See "Bird Diets," Part II of this volume. Weed seeds or grass seed (untreated with chemical) are yet another good source of nutrition.

2. T.J. Lafeber, D.V.M., *Tender Loving Care For Pet Birds*, p. 17.

Fruits, vegetables and greens should be sectioned, sliced or chopped into appropriate sizes for your bird.

bird. He will chew or peck at this for his snacks, once his given amount of seed is gone. Depending on his species, your bird may prefer the fruit, vegetable or greens over his seed mix.

Some owners think that if they give their bird too much in the way of fruit or greens, it will cause diarrhoea. This is not entirely true. Fresh produce will not cause diarrhoea if eaten regularly. Although the droppings take on a greenish colour and tend to be a little more liquid, this simply reflects the properties of the food itself, which contains more water, and therefore produces more urine. If a bird is fed greens only on occasion, he will eat voraciously and this overindulgence can cause the diarrhoea.

Ripe fruits and vegetables should not consist of more than 25% of the bird's total diet, and everything should be thoroughly washed to remove all traces of insecticide. Here is a good rule of thumb: any fruit, vegetable or green that you can eat, your bird can also eat, quite safely.

One easy, convenient source of greens is the bird's own seed. To germinate the seed, "take the volume that you want to sprout and soak it in water for a period of time relative to the environmental temperature. If the temperature approaches 38°C (100°F), the length of soaking time is 3 to 5 hours; if 4°–10°C (40°–50°F), 6 to 8 hours, or overnight soaking is required. Then rinse them well, and place in a warm, dark area to allow germination to take place. Rinse and drain every 6 to 12 hours to keep them moistened, and to prevent the seeds from going sour (fermenting). When the sprouts reach about 1.2 cm (½ in.) in length, they can be fed. Store the sprouted seed in the refrigerator to stop further sprouting until they are used"[3]. Do not feed sprouted seed if it is mouldy.

Actually, this is an excellent method for testing the nutritional value of your bird's seed. If it does not germinate in 3 to 4 days, the seed's quality is

3. Greg J. Harrison, D.V.M. Personal correspondence.

poor, and you should look for a new source.

You can also plant the bird seed in a bit of earth, though the latter should be free of chemical fertilizer. Use small flower pots and plant in them every 4 or 5 days, so that you always have a new pot of growth coming along for the bird.

Another easy source of greens is the occasional piece of grass sod placed in the cage, but again make sure is it clean sod, untreated by chemicals.

These greens are recommended: broccoli, brussel sprouts, swiss chard, collards, spinach, kale, carrot tops, celery leaves and stalks, cabbage, endive, mustard greens, chickweed, dandelions and green tree branches. Lettuce does not contain much nutrition, but leaf and bibb lettuce are better than head lettuce or romaine. You may even try freezing greens in season for later use.

FOOD VARIETY

Some birds will not take to a variety of foodstuffs easily. Birds are generally resistant to change and may take weeks or even months to accept new foods. If your bird does not appear to be eating the new things you offer, persevere and you will be rewarded.

Above all, be patient with your bird and be gentle. Introduce the new in a calm, quiet manner that does not seem threatening.

Birds are robust little creatures, but they are suspicious by nature. A strange food product in its seed cup may frighten a bird so badly that it will shun the cup entirely. Even slight changes in the size, shape and colour of

Birds should be encouraged to try new foods.

dishes, or their contents, may put some birds right off their food and water. A bird that will not eat can die in as little as 48 hours, simply because its high metabolic rate requires a steady source of nutrition and energy. Thus, it is very important, when introducing new things to the cage, that you make certain the bird continues to eat and drink.

In general, birds can eat whatever their owners eat, providing the food is wholesome. Here are some suggestions: cooked egg yolk, cheeses, brown or whole wheat bread (with butter, peanut butter or jam), breakfast cereals, crackers, pound cake or similar products, pasta (pizza, macaroni), cookies, baby foods and cooked meat.

GRIT

Since birds do not have teeth for chewing their food, they have developed a very muscular organ in their digestive tracts, which helps grind their food into smaller, more digestible particles. This organ is called the gizzard. An abrasive material like grit is required by most birds to assist the gizzard in its grinding action.

Authorities do not agree on the universal need for grit. Some claim that species husking their seeds (eating the seed only and not the husk) digest their food efficiently, whether grit is present or not[4]. Others say grit is essential to any bird's health. Most seed-eating birds in the wild depend on grit to aid digestion, so it should be provided to them in captivity.

Choose a grit size relative to the size of your bird.

---

4. Lafeber, p. 13.

Ground-up oyster shell and egg shell added to the grit becomes an extra source of minerals in the diet. (Use the white oyster shells; some authorities believe that the grey or dark shells contain too much lead.) If your bird does not eat his cuttle bone or mineral block, you can crush these up and add it to the mixture.

Grit should also consist of a hard, insoluble stone like crushed quartz; its sharp edges will aid the grinding action of the gizzard.

I do not advise the addition of charcoal to the grit, as is found in some commercial mixtures. Reportedly, the charcoal removes vitamins A, B_2 and K from the intestine, thus contributing to vitamin deficiency.

Birds only require a limited amount of grit (just enough to fill a small treat cup) because of the lengthy time these grains stay in the gizzard. Monthly or quarterly offerings for large birds are considered sufficient by a number of authorities. For smaller birds, I recommend offering grit on a free choice basis. Use a grit size relative to the size of your bird: small for small birds, medium for medium-sized birds and coarser grains for the larger birds.

Place the grit or gravel in a small container and attach it above the floor of the cage rather than spreading it all over the cage floor. The latter method is wasteful and expensive, since the bird's droppings continually foul the mixture.

VITAMINS

A high percentage of pet birds are vitamin and mineral deficient. This figure may run as high as 80% because too many bird owners are uninformed about what constitutes a proper diet for their pets.

All birds require certain vitamins and minerals in their diet; if this intake does not occur daily, then deficiencies will result. Even the bird owner who carefully provides a variety of food stuff can end up with a problem bird, especially if that bird is a finicky eater.

The right vitamin mixture contributes a solid base to your bird's health, but any old mixture will not do. You should look for the combination of vitamin types that is specifically recommended for birds, whose requirements are different from those of animals. The chart on page 57 indicates these particular vitamins, and their respective values to the bird's health. Use this chart as a guide the next time you are selecting an appropriate vitamin mixture for your bird. Read the label carefully.

While it is advisable to give your bird a vitamin supplement on a daily basis, it will not be easy. Vitamin powders are very difficult to get into a bird. If you try mixing the powder with the seed, it only settles to the bottom of the cup or adheres to the outer seed shells, which simply fall away and are never consumed. Put the powder in water, and it makes an insoluble paste that the bird will not go near. Your best bet is a liquid vitamin-mineral mixture that can be given directly to the bird, put on his fruit and vegetables, or dissolved in his water.

Vitamin Chart[5]

Vitamin	Function(s)	Effect(s) of Deficiency
A	essential for: tissue growth and regeneration; eyesight. Keeps skin and bones healthy.	often causes mouth and throat lesions, and defects in eye function.
B1 Thiamine	assists: important metabolic functions: overall growth; the development of smooth muscle texture and a healthy nervous system.	commonly causes leg paralysis, poor appetite, digestive upset and general weakness
B2 Riboflavin	assists: important metabolic functions; skin, feather and nail quality.	produces "curly toe" paralysis.
B3 Niacin	important to: metabolic processes; nervous and digestive systems; production of hormones.	slow growth, poor feather quality and scaly dermatitis.
B6 Pyridoxine	assists: production of digestive juices; development of red blood cells and antibodies; operation of nervous and musculoskeletal systems.	decreased appetite and weight; impaired reproduction
B12 Cyanoco-balamin	essential for: normal metabolism.	impaired egg hatchability; bone deformities and growth retardation.
Biotin	assists: important metabolic functions.	impaired egg hatchability; bone deformities; skin disease.

5. Source((for vitamin & mineral charts) John D. Kirschmann, *Nutrition Almanac* (New York: McGraw-Hill, 1975) pp. 13–60,; C. Ivar Tollefson, "Nutrition," in *Diseases of Cage Aviary Birds*, ed. Margaret L. Petrak, V.M.D. (Philadelphia: Lea & Febiger, 1969), pp. 146–48.

Choline	assists: metabolizing of fats & cholesterol; functioning of the nervous system, liver and kidneys.	kidney and liver ailments; fatty liver degeneration; slipped tendon and hock disease.
Folic Acid	helps: the body use proteins; the production of red blood cells and body tissue.	anaemia, loss of feather colour, and retarded body and feather growth.
Pantothenic Acid	essential for: cellular metabolism; a healthy digestive tract; functioning of adrenal glands.	retarded growth and poor feather development; skin diseases; liver damage; impaired egg hatchability.
C	assists: connective tissue formation, and healing wounds and burns; production of red blood cells; fighting infection.	may cause scurvy in fruit and nectar eaters.
D3	essential for: bone formation; a healthy heart and nervous system; blood clotting (Birds do not utilize vitamin D_2; they must have D_3).	rickets; egg binding and soft egg shells.
E	is an antioxidant; prevents the degeneration of fatty acids, and vitamins A and B; increases fertility, blood circulation and tissue regeneration.	decreased fertility; degenerative muscle disease and softening of the brain; severe itchiness; glandular enlargement and edema.
K	essential for: proper liver functioning; blood clotting; vitality factor.	impaired blood clotting.

MINERALS

Mineral supplements are as important to your bird as vitamins because most seeds are mineral deficient, especially in calcium.

Calcium and phosphorus deficiencies can show up as a sudden lameness in female birds that are laying eggs. When the minerals stored in the mother's bones are utilized to form the egg shells, this extra demand causes a severe depletion of body reserves and a painful lameness results. Proper mineral supplementation usually corrects this problem.

Mineral deficiency can also cause the "splay-legged" condition shown in the photograph. This is a bone and joint deformity, known as rickets. Some 60% of these cases are caused by nutritional deficiencies in the diet that has been fed to the parents before the eggs are laid[6].

I have discovered that some of these baby birds can be saved from permanent deformity if the condition is treated in its early stages. The legs are hobbled together, and remain bandaged during the entire growth period. A proper diet must accompany this treatment, and the tapes can ultimately be removed when growth has stopped and the bones are firmer.

The chart on minerals (page 60) indicates those which a bird needs and thrives on. Some of the most common mineral supplements include: powdered minerals and ground up egg or white oyster shells (these can be added to the grit mixture), iodized mineral blocks, cuttle bones, and skim milk. A small amount of the latter can be added to the bird's water, but this water must be changed daily.

Unfortunately, many birds will not eat minerals in the forms normally provided. This is why a liquid preparation (as described above in the

A mineral deficiency in the diet of the parents can cause rickets in the young.

6. Other factors contributing to the deformity include: over-breeding, 20%; breeding old birds, 10%, and 10%, caused by genetic defects.

vitamin section) containing both vitamins and minerals comes highly recommended. When added to their drinking water, birds find the liquid supplement quite palatable, and you will have the assurance that your bird is ingesting all the vitamins and minerals it needs daily.

Mineral Chart

Mineral	Function(s)	Effect(s) of Deficiency
Calcium	development and growth of bones and muscles; proper functioning of heart, muscles, blood and nervous system.	poor bone growth, bone deformities and bones bend or fracture easily.
Chlorine	helps maintain chemical acid alkali and fluid balance; produces digestive stomach acids.	improper digestion; loss of body fluids; upset in acid alkali balance.
Iodine	acts as a regulator of metabolism; essential to thyroid production of thyroxine hormone.	enlarged thyroid and parathyroid glands (goitre); other impaired metabolic functions.
Iron	essential for the development and function of healthy blood; is part of the haemoglobin in red blood cells that transports oxygen.	causes anaemia and impaired transport of oxygen from the lungs to the tissue; muscle weakness; poor functioning of whole body.
Magnesium	important for bone formation and proper metabolism; activates enzymes.	impairment in bone formation; interference with the proper metabolism of carbohydrates and aminoacids.
Manganese	important for: bone and blood formation; regulating metabolism by activating enzymes.	bone disease; anaemia; interference with body metabolism; weakness.

Phosphorus	essential for: important metabolic functions; cell growth and regeneration; digestion of vitamins B2 and B3; combines with calcium in bone formation.	poor bone formation and bone disease; poor tissue healing and body sores.
Selenium	works in conjunction with vitamin E; may have some anti-cancer properties.	poor tissue healing; weakness of muscles.
Sodium	regulates the body's fluid balance and helps in acid alkali balance.	dehydration; upset in acid alkali balance.
Zinc	essential for: normal matabolism; is part of insulin.	upset in body metabolism; tendency towards diabetes mellitus due to decrease in insulin production.

WATER

Clean, fresh water must be provided for your bird daily, so that it can drink whenever it wants. Some birds, such as the canary, will die in as short a period as 48 hours if no water is available. Water dishes must be kept scrupulously clean, and so placed within the cage that contamination by droppings or food is minimal.

If birds are eating succulent fruits, vegetables and greens, they will be obtaining much of their water from these sources, and their drinking intake will be proportionately less.

FEEDING A BIRD FOOD FROM YOUR MOUTH

There are certain bacteria that are normal flora for humans and mammals such as E. coli, yet when they get into a susceptible bird can cause serious illness. A bird would usually have to be a bit run down and sickly for this to occur, but it is possible. Therefore it is not recommended to feed birds food directly out of your mouth.

5
Is Your Bird Sick

BIRD VETERINARIANS

Sometimes, despite all your precautions and diligence, your bird does get sick. This is when your close observation of the bird's usual behaviour becomes indispensable. Knowing your bird, you will immediately recognize that a change has occurred in his actions or appearance, and can report this deviation to your veterinarian.

You should be aware that not all veterinarians treat birds, or are equally knowledgeable in their diseases. It will be worth your while to seek out a veterinarian who is especially skilled in avian medicine. If you are a new bird owner, this type of veterinarian can start you off on the right foot, giving you the particular advice needed for your species of bird.

Have your pet examined by your "bird veterinarian" at least 2 to 4 times a year. He will trim the nails and beak if needed, and check the bird for symptoms of disease. He can often recognize early symptoms that you would not necessarily notice yourself, or he may wish to perform routine blood tests to help determine the state of your bird's health.

For the sake of convenience, you may sometimes be tempted to call your veterinarian and ask for a telephone diagnosis of your bird's symptoms. In so doing, you place the veterinarian in an awkward position: he wants to help, yet he cannot be certain that all the bird's symptoms have been rigorously observed. It is essential that he see and examine your bird in order to arrive at a correct diagnosis and confidently prescribe the right treatment.

Have your pet examined by your "bird veterinarian" at least 2 to 4 times a year.

When a trip to the veterinarian becomes necessary, take your bird in its own cage if possible, and do not clean the cage for 12 hours prior to your appointment, so that the doctor can examine the bird's droppings. Leave all dishes in the cage (remembering to empty the water dish). If your bird is sick, the doctor may want to hospitalize it, and he will need these dishes. He will also want to see samples of the bird's seed mixture and any medication it happens to be on[1].

Before carrying the cage outside to your car, cover it with a blanket to prevent chilling, and prewarm the car if the weather is cool. Birds can be transported safely in the cold winter months if these precautions are followed.

Often a veterinarian can offer constructive criticism, and even solve the bird's problem, when the cage environment is there to be examined along with the bird. Observing the bird in its own environment, before examination, also helps the veterinarian arrive at his diagnosis.

Don't Be Alarmed – It's Normal

After being examined by the veterinarian, your bird may pant like a dog and hold its wings away from the body. Birds are inclined to do this after a period of physical exertion or stress. This behaviour enables the bird to lower its body temperature when overheated. Normally, the body temperature is about 40.5°C (105°F).

As a general rule, I discourage "pet shop" medications for treating sick birds. You are jeopardizing your bird's health by relying on your own diagnosis, or that of the pet shop staff, and then choosing an over-the-counter medicine to treat a guessed-at disease. Neither you nor the pet shop staff are qualified to diagnose diseases or prescribe treatment. If the diagnosis is wrong and the prescribed medicine proves harmful, it may be too late for corrective therapy when the veterinarian finally does see the bird.

Early diagnosis and treatment is essential. Do not allow your bird to be sick more than two days before you seek professional help. The longer the bird is sick, the harder it is to treat and its chances of recovery are greatly reduced.

HOW YOU CAN HELP: 6 WAYS

There will be times when you cannot get your sick bird to a veterinarian immediately. In that brief waiting period, there are certain first aid measures you can take:

---

1. Robert Millard Stone, "Clinical Examination and Methods of Treatment," in *Diseases of Cage and Aviary Birds*, ed. Margaret L. Petrak, p. 177.

Keep the bird warm

This is most important. Raise the temperature in the bird's environment to 27–30°C (80–85°F). There are several ways to do this. You can heat the room the bird is occupying with an electric base board heater, or heat the cage itself. If the cage is not too large, set it on top of a towel-covered heating pad, and cover the entire cage with another towel, leaving only a narrow opening at the front of the cage. Put a thermometer in the cage (where big birds cannot destroy it), and turn the heating pad control to a setting that keeps the inside of the cage at 27–30°C (80–85°F). The back of the cage can also be covered with clear plastic wrap in order to let in light, while still maintaining the desired heat level.

A 60 watt light bulb is less effective than the heating pad, but still useful in a pinch. Set the light bulb about 30 cm (12 in.) from the open side of the otherwise covered cage. The heat from the bulb will warm the bird, although the constant light may interfere with its sleep. Remember, the bulb is a temporary measure to keep the bird warm until a heating pad can be obtained.

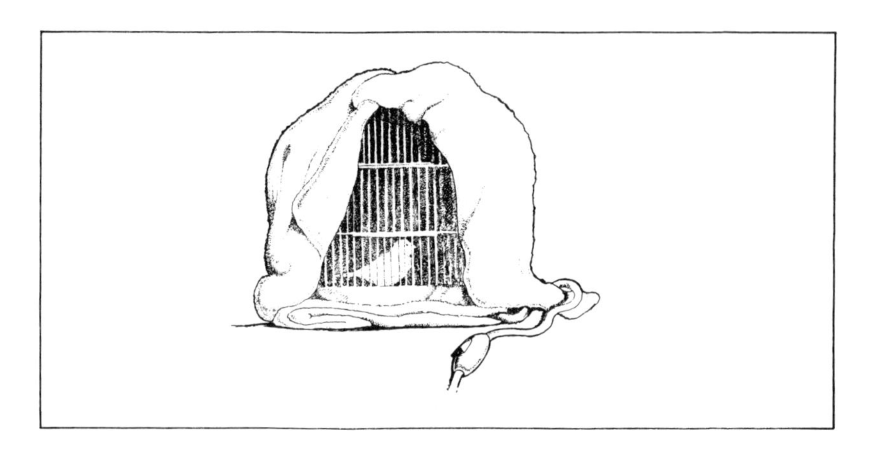

In an emergency, keep the bird warm.

Stop the bleeding

Birds cannot afford to lose much blood, especially the smaller species, so you must act quickly to stop any haemorrhaging.

If a pin feather is bleeding, pull it out and apply firm pressure to the wound with a dry cotton pad for a few minutes. If a toe nail is bleeding, rub a moistened styptic pencil on the bleeding area and again apply pressure with a piece of dry cotton until the bleeding stops. Stubborn bleeding may require heat cautery[2]. When the bleeding is from a skin wound, apply

2. For an explanation of this method, see p. 37.

pressure to the area, wrap the bird in a blanket or towel, and rush it to a veterinarian.

He must eat

A bird may have less than 48 hours to live if it will not eat. Be sure it does. Encourage your bird to take any kind of food it will eat, and place its food within easy reach. Hand feed the bird if need be.

Keep him quiet

Leave the bird to himself as much as possible; sick birds need far more undisturbed rest.

Eye injuries

For severely injured or infected eyes, first prevent the bird from aggravating the eye further by gently cleaning it with a piece of damp cotton, then apply a small amount of soothing eye drops or eye ointment. Human eye products can be used safely. To inhibit the bird's scratching, you may have to hold your pet when you take it to the hospital, or fit the bird with a wide Elizabethan collar.

Diarrhoea

For diarrhoea (not to be confused with polyuria or excess urinary output) put 5–15 drops (depending on the bird's size) of Kaopectate® per ounce of water in the bird's drinking water,[3] or give the bird boiled rice water after the water has cooled.

Do not give a laxative to your bird unless directed to do so by your veterinarian.

Do not give alcoholic products to your sick bird. A few drops of brandy or whisky will not cure the bird and may even kill it. If you must use whisky, drink it yourself.

Do not try to "play doctor" and treat the bird yourself, unless you are very experienced and know exactly what you are treating. A delay in proper treatment could cost the life of the bird.

Do not use human or pet shop medicines unless your veterinarian has specifically suggested these. Remember that your bird's life is at stake, so trust no one's diagnosis and prescription save that of your veterinarian. Birds must have the right drug for the particular disease, administered in the proper dosage. Too much medicine may kill it, and too little will do nothing to help.

---

3. Kaopectate® is a human diarrhoea product manufactured by Upjohn Company of Canada, Don Mills, Ontario.

SIGNS AND SYMPTOMS OF A SICK BIRD

Birds are sturdy, enduring creatures and in the early stages of a disease you may not notice the subtle symptoms they show unless you are very observant. Often the bird has been sick for some time, indeed is critically ill, before it shows a more pronounced symptom that finally catches your attention. These charts will help you recognize different signs that are symptomatic of a sick bird. Remember that any deviation from the normal routine can signal illness. If you are in doubt, have your bird checked over.

Symptoms To Watch For

Eye Discharge — *the bird may be discharging from an eye, or the eyelid may be partly closed.*
This could indicate a sore, infected eye, and could even be part of a generalized infection or disease.

Nasal Discharge — *moisture or "caking" around one or both nostrils, which may become plugged.*
You may see a crusting of the feathers just above or around the nostrils. This is discharge that has dried and built up in the feathers. The word "cold" should not be used in reference to respiratory problems in birds. The human "cold" is a specific virus disease that does not affect birds.

Crusty Build-up — *around the beak, face or legs.*
It is most common in budgies and could indicate the presence of parasites called cere mites; this disease needs immediate veterinary treatment, or the beak can become permanently deformed.

Laboured Breathing — *usually a symptom of respiratory distress (the birds needs immediate attention).*
— *the tail may be bobbing up and down with each breath.*
These symptoms can indicate respiratory problems, or serious internal problems in the abdominal cavity.

Sneezing — *varies from a quiet "choo" to a little "click", or a pronounced sneeze with shaking of the head.*
You may see little droplets of moisture sprayed onto a mirror or into the air. Sneezing indicates problems in the respiratory tract or sinuses.

Don't Be Alarmed – It's Normal

Birds may sneeze once or twice a day, and may even dig a toenail into a nostril to remove some irritant. Talking birds may mimic coughs or sneezes that they hear from their owners, and these noises should not be confused with a true sneeze or cough brought on by a respiratory infection.

Eating Less — *will be evident by fewer droppings.*

Weight Change — *becoming thinner and losing weight.*

Some interference in the digestive process may result in a bird eating normal or even extra amounts of food, yet still losing weight. A bird usually has to be examined more closely to ascertain the extent of weight loss. The breast bone or keel bone will protrude more as the muscle on either side of it decreases in size. For an accurate reading, the bird should be weighed on a gram scale.

– *getting fatter.*

Overweight or obese birds are not healthy, and should be checked.

Listlessness — *sitting with feathers fluffed out, body hunched over, head under its wing.*

The bird is feeling terrible and is telling you it needs help.

Feather Changes — *prolonged moulting; feathers look ragged and sparse.*

— *loss of feathers; the bird may be chewing or picking at them.*

— *extra long downy feathers that grow out beyond the rest.*

— *bare areas where feathers are not regrowing.*

Swelling — *unusual swelling or enlargements.*

Be sure to investigate any swellings that suddenly appear.

Increased Irritability — *an irritable bird is often an ill bird.*

Lameness — *favouring a foot or leg.*

Lameness can be caused by many different factors. It could be minor or very serious; it is better to have the leg checked than to be sorry later.

Change in Droppings — *loose or unformed stool.*

— *becoming lighter green or greyish in colour.*

Normally, stool is coiled and formed around a whitish urine centre; its colour is green to black. Normal stool will vary in colour and consistency depending on the type of food and amount of water consumed. Greens and fruit cause a looser, greener stool. Drier foods produce a firmer, formed stool.

— *excess clear or coloured liquid around a formed stool.*
This is not diarrhoea, but excess urine. It could indicate kidney disease.

— *a decrease in number.*
This indicates a decrease in food intake. A normal small bird will pass somewhere between 40 to 60 droppings in a 24 hour period. If it passes less than this, it is sick. Twenty stools or less per day means a critically sick bird.

— *showing red blood.*
This is symptomatic of bleeding in the lower bowel, urinary tract or cloaca.

— *showing black blood.*
This means bleeding in the upper digestive tract.

— *showing whole or undigested seeds.*
This indicates severe bowel problems.

— *showing excessive amounts of gravel or grit.*

— *being coarser in texture and larger in size.*
This means the digestion is incomplete.

— *no stools.*
The bird may be constipated, or a faecal mass may be adhering to the feathers, thus plugging the vent opening.

Don't Be Alarmed – It's Normal

When nervous or apprehensive, birds will defaecate frequently and their droppings will contain more watery urine.

Birds that are laying eggs will produce larger sized droppings because the cloaca is enlarged by the eggs' passage, and therefore, holds more faeces.

6
Common Diseases and Psychological Disorders

The purpose of this section is to review the most common problems and diseases to which birds are prone, so that my readers can recognize a disturbing situation before it goes too far. Any reader who wishes a detailed text on one or more species and their diseases will find suggestions for "Further Reading" in Part II of this edition.

SORE EYES

Your bird may suddenly begin to favour one or both eyes by holding the lids partly closed. This could be accompanied by a watery or pusy discharge that dries to form crusty material around the eyelid margin. The eyelids may be swollen, and the area around the eye inflamed and sore. Very often the bird will rub or scratch at the area, and the side of its face may even become swollen. The bird itself may look fluffed and listless.

Listless, fluffed up, eyes half closed: the classic symptoms of a sick bird.

Eye infections can occur in isolation, or as part of a more serious systematic infection. For instance, advanced sinusitis creates soreness and swelling both in the eye and its surrounding area. Sinusitis with severe eye involvement is usually unilateral (one-sided), but can be bilateral on occasion. Only your veterinarian can differentiate these complications. For the best results, your bird must be treated in the early stages of this disease.

CERE PROBLEMS

The cere is the raised skin area surrounding some bird's nostrils. It is quite prominent in certain species like budgies, hawks and falcons, and absent in species like canaries and finches. This part of the bird's body can fall prey to

Brown hypertrophy of the cere.

the crusty formations caused by cere mites[2]. However, the disease responds well to treatment, providing professional help is sought before the weakened area (the beak) becomes misshapened and permanently deformed.

You should also be aware that tumours can occur in the cere area. Another cere problem quite common in budgies is an abnormality called brown hyperplasia, or hypertrophy of the cere. This condition changes the colour of the cere to a dark or medium brown. The brown layer gradually builds up, thickens, and if not removed, it will eventually block the nostrils, forming a horn-like protrusion from the cere. It is often associated with chronic poor health and ageing, and can be one of the symptoms seen in hypothyroid disease. It is more common in females than males. Frequent removal of this brown build-up is recommended, and a whole-hearted effort should be made to improve the nutrition and health of the bird.

TOPOGRAPHY OF A FINCH

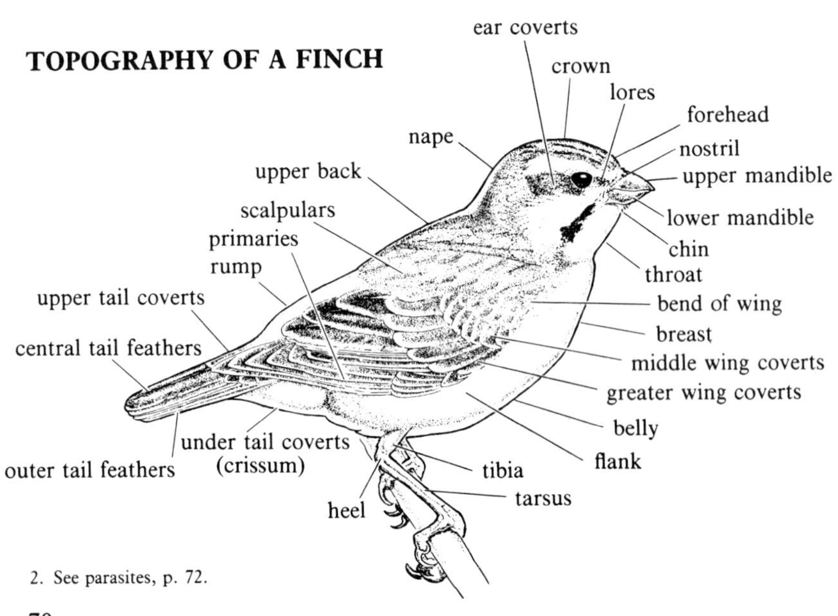

2. See parasites, p. 72.

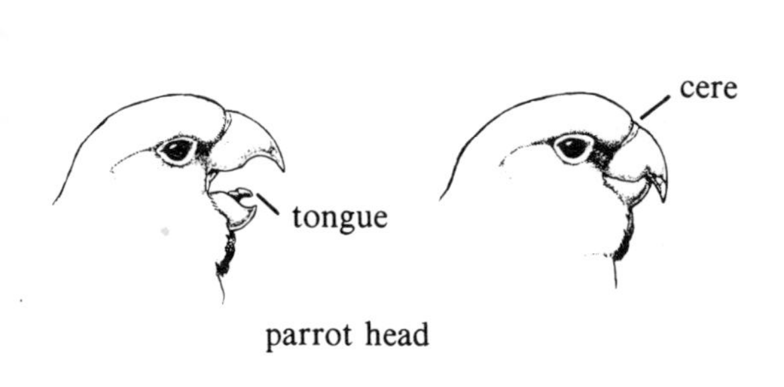

parrot head

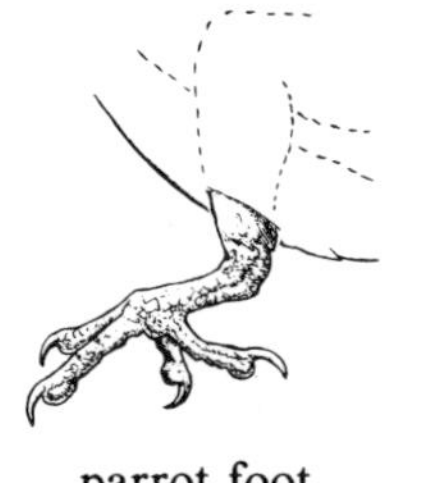

parrot foot
(note: two toes
pointed forward,
and two pointed back)

REGURGITATION AND VOMITING

Regurgitation is the process by which a bird voluntarily brings food material up from the crop in order to feed another bird. The regurgitated material consists of seeds and other material that has been eaten, plus a little mucus, which binds everything together. A budgie will often regurgitate in front of a shiny surface where it sees the image of its own face, and so, believes it is feeding another bird. It will also make this offering to other budgies in the same cage. This is a normal phenomenon and should not be cause for concern. If a bird regurgitates to excess, remove its mirror and it will usually stop.

A parrot may regurgitate as a form of affectionate welcome when greeted by its owner. This practice is associated with the feeding of its mate or young, and is brought on by a combination of psychological, hormonal and visual stimuli. The bird will extend its head and neck a few times, and present its owner with a nice gift of food. This is also normal.

Vomiting is quite a different matter. This is an involuntary process in which the bird mainly brings up mucus and some food. It happens because the bird is sick. The bird will often be fluffed up, listless and droopy; mucus will be stuck to the feathers of the head because of the bird's tendency to shake itself as it vomits, and then tries to get rid of the mucus. A bird behaving in this manner should be professionally examined.

SINUSITIS

This disease may be found by itself, or in conjunction with a respiratory disease.

Sinusitis often shows up as a swollen, weeping eye; sneezing, with or without nasal discharge, and swelling at the sides of the face. Chronic, mild sinusitis with a slight sneeze and nasal discharge is commonly found in cage birds, and specific treatment is required to correct it.

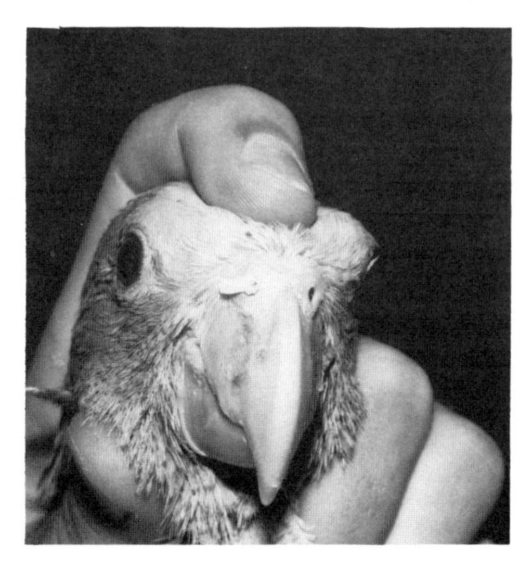

Example of sinusitis (note the blocked nostril) in a parrot.

Cere or Knemidocoptic mite (below).

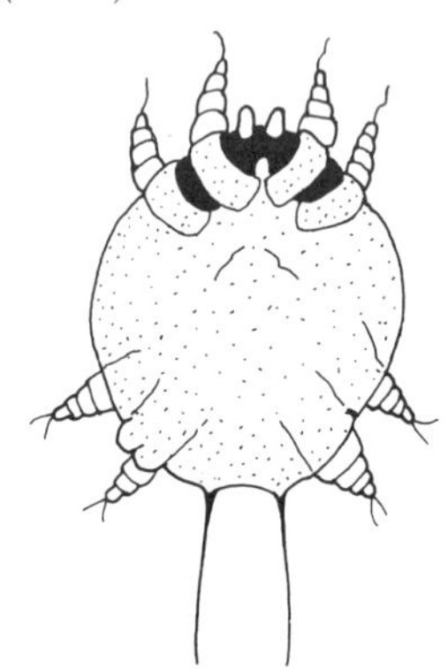

RESPIRATORY PROBLEMS

If a bird is subjected to draughts or a sudden drop in temperature, it could develop one of several respiratory disease problems. The trouble may begin as an upper respiratory infection involving the nasal passages, upper throat, pharynx and possibly the sinuses. If not treated, it can progress into the lungs and cause pneumonia, or make its way into the air sacs, which can cause death.

Early symptoms include sneezing, nasal discharge and listlessness. As the problem grows worse, the bird fluffs up and goes off its food. The signs of laboured breathing get progressively worse until the tail is bobbing at each breath. Later, weight loss is evident; the bird weakens, stays at the bottom of its cage and eventually dies.

When close observation of your bird leads you to suspect a respiratory illness, it is important to have the bird examined and treated within two days of noticing the early warning signs. Do not wait too long in the hope that "it will be better tomorrow".

PARASITES

Internal parasites are uncommon in cage birds. If you suspect the presence of these (because of diarrhoea, listlessness or weight loss) take a fresh faecal sample and one or more of the parasites (if they are visible) to your veterinarian for identification and prescribed treatment.

External parasites are the more common. Of these, you are likely to see the cere, red or grey, and feather mites.

Cere or Knemidocoptic Mites – mainly infest budgies and are usually

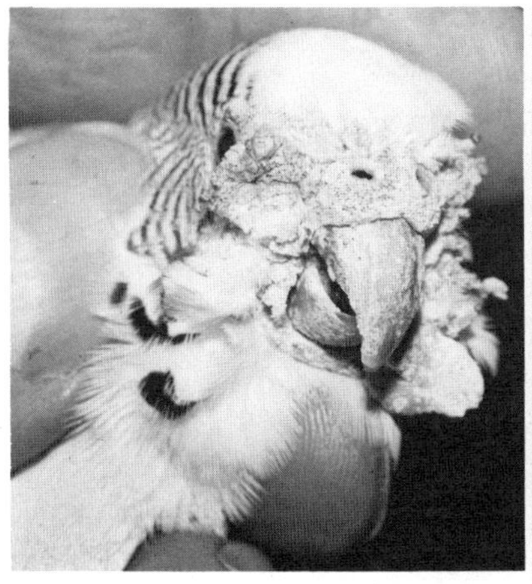
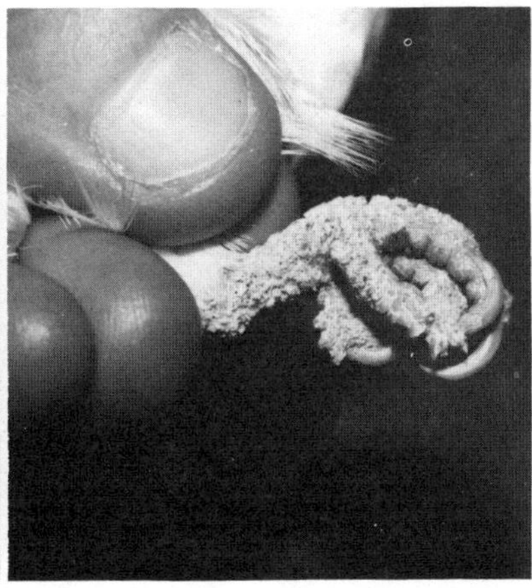

Cere mites infesting the face and feet of a budgie.

found around the cere, the sides of the face and beak, on the eyelids, on the legs and feet, and around the vent area. They form a thick, extensive crust, and on close examination, the observer will see the tiny holes that give the crust its honeycomb appearance. These tiny holes are the burrows of the mite.

The common name for this disease is "Scaly Face" or "Scaly Leg". If it is treated promptly by your veterinarian, the disease responds quickly to treatment and there will be no permanent damage to the beak.

Red or Grey Mites – are found sometimes on the bird, sometimes in his cage. These mites usually hide in the cage by day and come out at night to feed on the bird. Birds are irritated and itchy when these mites are present. The mites can be detected by covering the cage with a white cloth at night, and later looking on the cloth's underside with a flashlight. You can keep these parasites away by thoroughly scrubbing the cage and its contents weekly, and having your veterinarian treat the bird for mites.

Feather Mites – attack the feather shafts, causing broken and damaged feathers. It is this damage that can drive a bird to feather-picking.

The occurrence of feather mites is a rarity, but they do show up from time to time. The mites can be seen by taking a scraping of the skin, which includes the base of the thickened feather shaft, and examining this under a suitable microscope.

Feather mites are best treated by hanging a pest strip in the bird's room for alternating periods of time. Hang it up for three days, then, remove it for three days. Repeat this procedure until the mites are dead. Do not leave the pest strip up for a prolonged period of time, or it may become toxic to the bird. This treatment should be conducted under the supervision of a veterinarian.

Balding disease as seen in canaries.

BALDING DISEASE

This disease is prevalent in canaries. The feather loss (alopecia) starts behind the neck and spreads up the back of the head, sometimes balding the entire surface. The skin often becomes thickened or scaly, and if this condition spreads to the eyelids, it may pose a physical problem for the bird. Generally, the balding does not affect a bird's health, except to make him more vulnerable to the cold. But the overt nature of the condition and its unsightliness tend to alarm the bird's owner.

In some cases the disease is caused by fungus or bacterial skin infections; more often, the cause remains a mystery. When balding occurs in male birds, they sometimes recover completely through male hormone treatments. But while the dermatitis is relatively easy to control, most of these birds remain permanently bald because the feather follicles have stopped generating new feathers. It is thought that certain hereditary factors may also contribute to this permanent baldness.

On occasion, baldness in canaries is the result of an arrested moult. Birds that are "stuck in moult" lose the feathers on their heads and necks, but do not grow replacements. The usual cause of this phenomenon is stress: perhaps the hen has been forced into egg-laying through too rich a diet; babies may have been put through the stress of training before they finished their baby moult. Even sudden changes in the weather can disturb or stress a bird enough to interrupt its normal moult cycle.

If possible, try to isolate the condition that is stressing your bird, and then get rid of it. Overbreeding may be one of these factors. To help a bald bird recover, try placing it in a flight cage (a large, roomy cage), and see if the feathers will regrow with the next moult.

FRENCH MOULT

The term French moult is often misapplied to a heavy moult, or a feather-picking condition. "French Moult is, primarily, a disease of young budgerigars, although it has also been reported in the young of lovebirds and other birds of the family psittacine[3]."

The disease is confined to baby birds. It is characterized by an inability to grow normal feathers, particularly the wing and tail feathers, which are shed before they can mature. Some birds have a severe form of the disease and never do grow normal feathers, but continue to moult their bent and twisted ones. When a milder form of the disease occurs, the bird will begin to grow normal looking feathers after 1 or 2 moults.

French moult as seen in a young budgie.

A great deal of effort has gone into researching the causes of this feather problem; still, a definitive theory has yet to emerge[4]. A virus factor is one among many of the speculative causes.

TUMOURS OR NEOPLASMS

Tumours or neoplasms (abnormal new growths) may afflict any species, but it is the budgies that seem most susceptible to these growths. The tumour masses can occur in all parts of the body. They consist of tissue cells that start to grow at random, forming a mass of tissue or a "lump".

There are two basic types of tumours. The benign type is characterized by slow, localized growth. The malignant or cancerous tumour is fast growing. It spreads rapidly to other parts of the body, particularly the lungs and liver, and will eventually cause the death of the bird unlucky enough to develop it.

The most common of the benign tumours found in budgies are lipomatous tumours that develop in the fatty tissue under the skin of the chest or abdomen. The beak is another area susceptible to benign growths, especially around its corners; the tumour that develops here is called a "papilloma".

When budgies develop malignant growths, they tend to be kidney

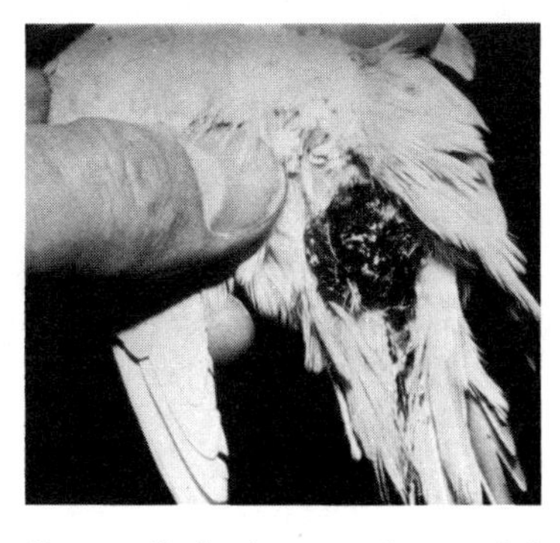

Severe oil gland tumour in an adult budgie.

3. T. Geoffrey Taylor, "French Moult," in *Diseases of Cage and Aviary Birds*, ed. Margaret L. Petrak, p. 237.

4. Taylor, p. 237.

tumours. These tumours cause a partial paralysis of one or both feet, and the bird will suddenly lose its ability to grasp the perch. Further leg paralysis is caused by the enlarged kidney putting pressure on the nerves that supply the leg. The stricken bird will also show symptoms of polyuria, weight loss and distension of the abdomen.

At the first sign of abnormal enlargements or swellings, your bird should be examined by a veterinarian before the growth gets too big. Small neoplasms are often quite easy to remove, but large masses are much harder, both on the bird and on the surgeon.

Don't Be Alarmed – It's Normal

You've noticed swelling in your bird's crop? No need to worry. When a bird eats, the crop becomes very distended as it fills up. Some people may confuse this with a fluctuating growth.

THYROID HYPERTROPHY

Thyroid hypertrophy can be found in any species, but is most common in budgies. The disease, also called "goitre", is an enlargement of the thyroid gland, which is located in the neck at the base of the "V" of the clavicle (or wish bone). Since the bird's vocal cords are close by, the expanding thyroid gland exerts pressure on both the vocal cords and the trachea (or wind pipe). As this pressure increases the bird begins to "squeak" with each breath, and its breathing becomes laboured. The squeaking and harsh breathing will be more pronounced when the bird is stressed by the effort of flight, or the trauma of being handled. Vomiting may also ensue when the oesophagus becomes so constricted that it interferes with the crop emptying properly.

Treated early enough, this disease will respond to an iodine supplement, and can even be prevented by giving the bird an iodized mineral block. If your bird ignores its mineral block, see your veterinarian for the right type of iodine to add to its water; tincture of iodine is not recommended. A 5% lugol's iodine should be used: one drop in the water daily or every two days.

HYPOTHYROIDISM

Budgies are more prone to hypothyroidism than other species. Mild or early forms of the disease can cause a thickening and browning of the cere; this is referred to as brown hypertrophy or hyperplasia of the cere[5].

5. Note that these cere changes can be caused by other factors.

An advanced case of hypothyroidism.

Progression of the disease will show up as abnormal growth of the down feathers, beginning with those under the wings. The down feathers grow longer than the regular feathers, and an advanced case will have fluffy down feathers sticking out all over its body. Other symptoms of impaired metabolism will follow as the disease gets worse; for instance, a high percentage of hypothyroid birds are obese. An untreated bird eventually dies.

Hypothyroidism is the result of the bird's thyroid gland producing insufficient amounts of the hormone, thyroxine. Treatment involves replacing this deficiency for the rest of the bird's life. The bird's food intake must also be carefully regulated to control the obesity.

OBESITY

This can become a serious medical problem in birds. Budgies seem to be the main species affected, but other species can be susceptible. In my experience, most birds with this problem have hypothyroid disease. But there are the few that are simply fat from overeating. The condition is easy to detect. As it gets fatter, the bird flies with more difficulty, and the effort leaves it out of breath. The greater weight eventually means it cannot fly at all.

Treatment usually involves thyroid supplementations, additional vitamins and minerals, and a strict dietary programme that controls caloric intake. Regular weights are recorded to monitor the bird's progress, and often the result is a reasonably healthy bird. However, treatment must continue throughout the bird's life, and should be conducted under a veterinarian's supervision.

An obese budgie.

KIDNEY DISEASE OR NEPHRITIS

When the kidneys are functioning improperly, the bird will often excrete an excessive amount of urine. The bird will be fluffed, listless, or off its food as the disease progresses. But in the early stage, excess urine and an increased thirst (polydipsia) may be the only symptoms.

Excessive urine (polyuria) is often misdiagnosed as diarrhoea. Diarrhoea can be secondary to a bad kidney problem, but the usual early symptom is polyuria. On close inspection of the polyuric droppings, you will see that

From left to right: regular stool; polyuria; diarrhoea.

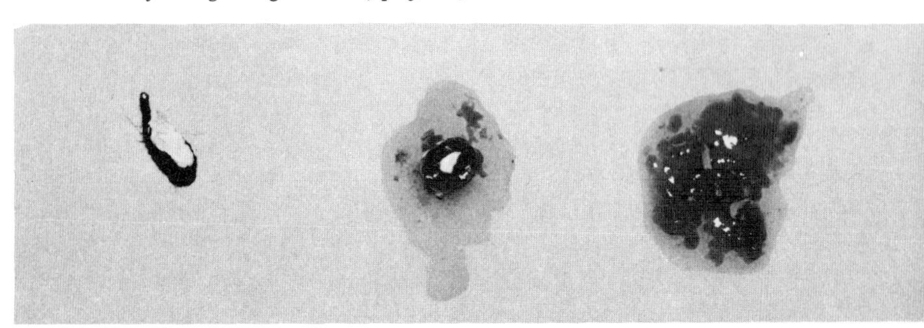

the stool mass is formed normally in the centre of a blob of water that may be clear, whitish, greyish or greenish-white in colour. The amount of water present will vary. The bird usually drinks a lot more water to replace the amount of water the diseased kidneys are excreting.

There are many causes of kidney disease, including infections, toxic substances and complications from other diseases. Malignant tumours are the common cause of kidney problems in budgies. If you notice the symptoms already described in your bird, have it treated promptly.

GOUT

Gout is caused by the body's failure to eliminate nitrogenous waste materials from the blood, via the kidneys. The result is the accumulation of urates and related substances in various parts of the body. Birds suffer two different forms of this disease: visceral and articular gout.

In visceral gout, the urates are deposited in and around the major internal organs. Articular gout takes a more obvious form. The urates are deposited in the joints of the limbs, particularly in the feet and legs, and the birds usually become painfully crippled. Lesions show up as whitish swellings around the joints.

A case of articular gout.

A diet characterized by a protein imbalance and vitamin-mineral deficiency is one traceable cause of gout. Most birds do not respond to treatment because of permanent kidney damage, but some have been known to recover when their dietary deficiencies are corrected.

DIARRHOEA

When the stool part of the dropping is loose and unformed, this is called diarrhoea. The stool may also be light green or greyish in colour. Diarrhoea has several causes: bacterial, viral, fungus or yeast infections; parasites; and mouldy, toxic or abrasive foods. It may also be a secondary problem to some other disease in the kidney, liver, or pancreas.

Proper diagnosis and treatment should be given as soon as possible to correct the situation before it grows worse.

OIL GLAND PROBLEMS

The oil gland (preening or uropygial gland) is situated above the base of the tail. It produces an oily secretion, traditionally thought to be a waterproofing substance, and a health aid to feather maintenance. Using their heads and beaks, birds spread the gland's secretion over their feathers when they groom themselves.

This gland is no longer considered essential to the bird or the feathers, nor has its surgical removal had any adverse effects. In fact, there are a number of birds, including many parrots and a few wild species like pigeons, woodpeckers and ostriches that do not have the gland at all.

Budgies and canaries seem to have more problems in this area than any other species, even though the oil gland generally tends to be vulnerable to disease. It can become distended from blockage of the little duct openings, or infection may get into an irritated gland and form an abscess. Occasionally, tumours will grow from this area and require surgical removal.

Some birds rub their heads on the base of their tails, or seem to pick at this area a lot. They may simply be spreading the preen gland secretions over their feathers. However, when a bird shows irritation and is constantly working at this rear area with its beak, it should be examined for abnormalities and treated if need be.

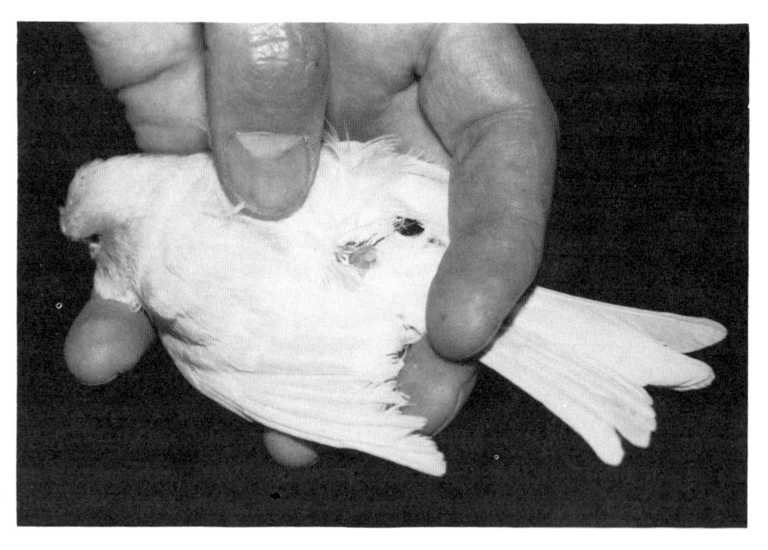

The oil gland in a canary.

EGG-BINDING

Female birds start their egg production in the ovary. What begins as a small yolk gradually enlarges and enters a tubular passage called the oviduct. Here the egg white and shell are added. Through muscular contractions, the egg gradually moves down the oviduct to the communal passage called the cloaca; here the digestive, urinary and reproductive systems meet, and empty through the vent or anal opening.

Egg-binding occurs when there is some abnormal interference in the passage of the egg, and the bird cannot lay the egg without help. This painful condition could have any number of causes: deficiencies in the diet; obesity; an inflamed, diseased oviduct; lack of muscle tone in the oviduct or abdominal wall; an extra large or misshapened egg; overbreeding; a bird starting to lay late in life; lack of a suitable place to lay the eggs, and the physical stress caused by cold or dampness.

Such a bird is often found at the bottom of its cage, fluffed up and listless. Perhaps it has stopped eating altogether; its lower abdomen is usually distended, and the bird may actually be seen straining to pass the egg. You may be tempted to put oil on the bird, hoping to lubricate the rear end, but the oil slick on the feathers will only contribute to the chilling of your bird. Rather, the bird must be kept warm 30°C (85°F), and taken to your veterinarian as soon as possible.

FRACTURES

Bone fracture in birds is quite a common orthopaedic problem. When the cage bird breaks a limb it is more likely to be the leg, whereas wild birds experience a higher number of wing fractures.

Fractures in small birds can usually be repaired, although breaks high up on the leg are difficult to immobilize. The two fractured ends of bone must be set into normal position, and then held in place by some form of splint.

Bone fractures in larger birds are much harder to heal, simply because the

Great Horned Owl with splinted wing.

African Grey Parrot wearing Elizabethan collar.

bird is so aggressively resistant to treatment. It is difficult to keep a splint on such a creature. Birds of the parrot family in particular are quite intolerant of any foreign material like a splint or cast, and will rip it away with their powerful beaks. To keep the splint intact, it may be necessary to fit the bird with a strong Elizabethan collar (a wide brim collar), which effectively prevents him from reaching the splinted area. However, these collars can be frustrating to the bird because they somewhat impair its ability to eat and drink. The smaller birds are much more tolerant of these collars.

A leg fracture can be spotted quite easily. The bird will be favouring its leg, which either hangs uselessly or bends at an odd angle. Wing fractures are not as common to the cage bird, but they certainly occur. A fractured wing is usually held in a drooping position when the wings are closed, and very often, the healed wing will cause some flying disability to the bird.

These cases must be taken to a veterinarian as soon as possible. Neglected or improperly treated fractures can result in severe deformities, so have your bird examined and treated if you suspect a fracture.

SORE FEET

Birds spend most of their time standing, and this subjects their feet to a lot of strain. Consequently, any disease problems to do with the feet will cause the bird great discomfort, and can even immobilize it.

As was mentioned in the section on perches[6], special care should be taken

An advanced case of hyperkeratosis in a finch.

6. See p. 19.

to give the bird a variety of perch sizes, shapes and textures in order to keep the feet as healthy as possible. One texture that must be avoided is sandpaper. Used as a slip-on perch cover, this abrasive material wears down the protective skin on the bottom of the foot and creates a raw area that is very painful. This ulcerous condition is sometimes called "bumble foot". Since the bird continually walks on these sores, the wounds become more and more irritated. Often your veterinarian will have to apply a bandage to protect the area while healing takes place.

Broken, bleeding toenails can be another painful foot problem that is easily avoided by keeping your bird's toenails trimmed regularly. Birds can also develop impairment in the circulation to one or more toes. This may have its cause in a thread or cloth fibre that has wrapped itself around the toe; the strangled toe turns purple and black, and then gangrene sets in. Sometimes the bird will chew at these dead toes, and they will have to be amputated by your veterinarian.

An accumulation of droppings on the feet may have the same grim result because the build-up interferes with blood circulation to the toes, and this causes gangrene. A similar scaly build-up can occur when successive layers of dead skin accumulate on the bird's feet and legs. This condition is called hyperkeratosis, and it is most commonly seen in canaries.

In hyperkeratosis, the build-up of dead skin can become so thick and crusty that the feet eventually crack. Secondary bacterial infection invades the cracked skin, causing the feet and legs to become very swollen and sore. This thickened build-up, whether of dead skin or droppings, must be carefully removed at regular intervals in order to maintain healthy feet and legs. When you or your veterinarian have removed the crusty scales, massage a vanishing-cream-base ointment[7] into the feet and legs. The cream will soften the skin and make your bird more comfortable.

Oily products should not be used to treat hyperkeratosis[8]. Even vanishing cream must be used sparingly, or the excess will spread out and cake up the feathers. The right ointment is available from your veterinarian; he or she should be the one to treat the bird's feet if you see them starting to swell and look sore.

CHLAMYDIOSIS (PSITTACOSIS, ORNITHOSIS OR PARROT FEVER)

This is a disease caused by the organism Chlamydia psittaci. It is important for bird owners to be aware of this disease as it is directly transmissible from

7. Such as HibitaneTM, an anti-bacterial ointment in a vanishing cream base. Manufactured by Ayerst Laboratories, Montreal, Quebec.

8. See "Oil and Feathers Do Not Mix," p. 40.

birds to man. Since birds are being transported widely over various parts of the world, this disease is being recognized more frequently. Fortunately the infection is susceptible to the tetracycline family of antibiotics. Human fatalities are rare. It can be difficult to diagnose in live birds and the symptoms are variable. It is very important that sick birds are treated by a knowledgeable veterinarian, especially those recently imported or exposed to newly imported birds.

NEWCASTLE DISEASE – (VVND – VELOGENIC VISCEROTROPIC NEWCASTLE DISEASE)

This disease is caused by a highly contagious virus and is sometimes carried into the country by newly imported birds. Although not dangerous to humans, it is fatal to poultry and other birds and can cause tremendous financial losses to the poultry industry if it ever gets a start in domestic birds. It generally comes in in birds originating from Mexico, Central America, and South East Asia.[9] Several species of cage birds are affected by the virus which is often fatal. Once diagnosed, the governmental agencies of many countries will slaughter all diseased and exposed birds and quarantine the facilities for disinfection. As it is a highly fatal disease, any unusual sudden deaths should be examined by your veterinarian.

SMUGGLING BIRDS

The reason most countries have laws requiring the quarantining of imported birds is because of the two diseases just previously mentioned. It is essential to the health of local birds in the importing countries to try to keep these diseases out, especially Newcastle Disease. Birds can go through quarantine and still have Chlamydia which can be a potential public health hazard, but a Newcastle outbreak could be disastrous to the poultry industry. It is important to discourage the smuggling of birds for these reasons. Be wary of buying "cheap" birds at flea markets or through newspaper ads and insist on finding out how long the birds have been in your country and how they got there. Report known cases of smuggling to the proper government authorities.

FEATHER-PICKING

Feather-picking is more of a problem in the larger psittacine birds, but any bird that experiences too much stress may be driven to this extreme. The worst offenders are the African Grey parrot, the cockatoo and the cockatiel.

---

9. Clubb, Susan, D.V.M., "Viscerotropic Velogenic Newcastle Disease in Pet Birds", in Kirk, R, (ed.), *Current Veterinary Therapy VIII*, Philadelphia, W.B. Saunders, 1983, pp. 628–630.

A feather-picker will attack various parts of its body, and the condition often gets worse.

This problem begins with feather loss in localized areas such as the upper and lower chest, back, sides and wings. It gradually gets worse. Feather-picking is often mistaken for moulting, and may even coincide with a heavy moult. However, on close inspection it is discovered that the fallen feathers are not coming out whole, but instead are being bitten off near the skin, leaving a lot of downy feathers exposed. Some birds will go further and bite off all the feathers down to the bare skin, and even beyond, biting at their own flesh until they cause open sores.

The only way to cure feather-picking is to find its cause. While it can be the result of either feather and skin parasites, or some nutritional deficiency, more often the condition is created by stressful situations. Stress can result from boredom, insecurity lack of privacy, a cage too small, heavy moulting, lack of sleep or infrequent bathing. Some birds will react to these stresses by turning their frustration on themselves, by self-mutilation. While the problem of feather-picking is minor to begin with, it should be solved in the early stages before it becomes an incurable vice.

It may be difficult for you to pinpoint the exact cause of your bird's disturbed feelings. However, your awareness of all the possible causes will enable you to eliminate these one by one, checklist fashion.

A bird's boredom can be offset by revolving a rich variety of objects and toys through the bird's cage environment[10]. His investigation of these different objects will galvanize the bird's interest, which is particularly important in the larger, more intelligent bird[11]. Engage your bird's interest, keep him busy and he will never be bored.

The feeling of insecurity and vulnerability can be eased by a hiding or privacy box, which need only be a wooden box big enough for the bird to enter and turn around in. Equip the box with a perch, so that the bird can stand on it and look out the open doorway, but be sure to face the box opening away from the front of the cage. This gives your bird a separate, private place where he can go to "get away from it all".

---

10. See "Toys and Entertainment", p. 29.
11. William C. Dilger, "Behavioural Aspects," in *Diseases of Cage and Aviary Birds*, p. 20.

Privacy box.

Cage size and shape are also contributing factors to the psychological health of your bird[12]. Birds need room to move around, exercise and sport about with their playthings, so buy a cage for its practicality and usefulness to the bird, and not for its "pretty" looks.

Itchy skin can be yet another cause of feather-picking. On rare occasions, this irritation is caused by parasites like the feather mite, which eats away at the feather shafts, and the red or grey mite, which feeds off the bird's skin. But the more usual cause of skin itchiness is a heavy moult. Given the large number of new feathers that are growing in at once, and the itchiness that accompanies this burst of growth, the affected bird can turn into a feather-picker. In these circumstances, the bird could be treated with a cortisone product recommended by your veterinarian. As a last resort, you might consider fitting the bird with an Elizabethan collar until the new feathers have grown in.

The stress of insufficient sleep is often overlooked in the search for causes of feather-picking. In fact, a well-rested bird is better able to cope with the little irritations that come his way. Make sure your bird gets his needed 9 to 12 hours sleep per day, and try not to interfere with the cover-at-dusk, uncover-at-dawn routine of his sleeping and waking.

Dirty or unkempt feathers will certainly bother a bird; he will want to get rid of them. As a result, he becomes a feather-picker. Allow and encourage your bird to bathe frequently; this experience stimulates the bird to preen his feathers and groom them clean. With healthy feathers, he will be a happier bird.

It has also been discovered that an infection involving an internal organ may start a bird to feather-pick.

A picking problem in cockatiels where they pick their shoulders, under their wings, sides and legs, has been attributed in California, USA, to intestinal giardia infection. A lot of these birds stopped picking when the intestinal problem was treated.[13]

---

12. See earlier section on the cage environment, p. 11.

A recently recognized feather disease has been occurring in mainly young cockatoos with the sulphur-crested species most frequently affected. The feathers often take on a brownish tinge, become brittle, break easily and come out. The entire body is involved including the head which differentiates this problem from a true feather-picker which will have head and part of its neck in normal featheration. This cockatoo disease also involves the beak and sometimes the nails and causes them to split and erode. Treatment is usually unsuccessful and, although the cause is not yet entirely understood, it has been thought to be of viral origin. Both wild and captive birds have been affected.

Sexual frustration or a desire to mate may also be an important cause of feather-picking. This can be a very dominant stress factor. Birds' natural instincts tell them they should choose a mate, breed, build nests, and raise young, and when they are deprived of these natural drives this acts as a stress factor that can start some of them to feather-pick. Pairing a feather-picker with an appropriate mate and setting them up in a breeding environment *may* stop the problem. This may not be the final answer either, however, as the author has seen some paired birds feather-pick only during their breeding-reproductive period and leave themselves alone during the rest of the year.

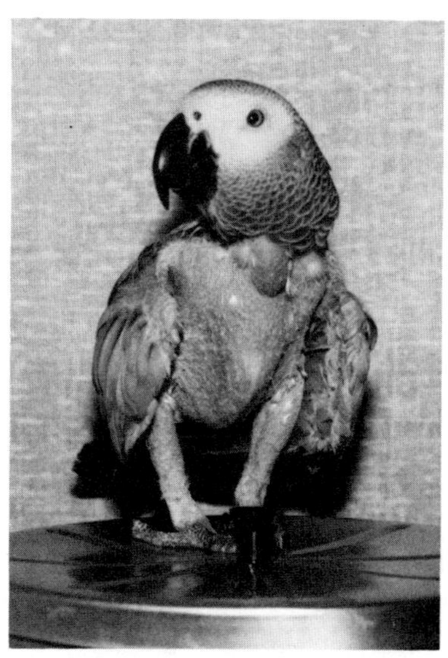

An incurable feather-picker.

The solution to feather-picking is not an easy one, and captivity itself is probably the biggest factor the bird has to deal with. Wild birds fly away from alarming or stressful situations and captive birds usually cannot do this.

Research on Feather-Picking

At his clinic in Burbank, California, Dr. Raymond Kray has been carrying on research with feather problem birds. In a recent publication of some of his findings, Dr. Kray sheds new light on the enigma of understanding and treating feather-pickers.[14] His case studies show a direct link between the area picked and its etiology or cause.

---

13. Personal communication with Dr. Alan Fudge, Avian Medical Centre of Sacramento, 6114 Greenback Lane, Citrus Heights, California, 95610, USA.
14. Dr. Raymond A. Kray, "Feather Problems," *Bird World* December–January 1981, pp. 4–7.

Kray divides feather problems into two categories: physiological (resulting from an internal disorder), and auto (or self-willed) mutilation. Birds suffering from the latter, masochistic syndrome will either shear or pluck away their feathers. The sheared feathers are bitten off, usually leaving the downy under feathers intact; but the birds that are driven to pluck themselves pull their feathers out entirely.

Kray concluded that this auto or self-mutilation is zonal in nature. In other words, the reason for the feather-picking becomes apparent from the area that has been picked. For instance, Kray notes this correlation between body zones and the cause of shearing or plucking:

Damage Zones	Cause
(a) **total body, except primaries** (b) **breast and thighs** (c) **breast, thighs and abdomen**	These birds are sexually activated, ready to breed and nest; especially African Grey parrots, cockatoos, conures and cockatiels.

Once sexed, paired and given suitable nesting areas, these birds usually begin to breed and stop mutilating their feathers within a month.

Dr. Kray goes on to list a number of correlations between body zones and the etiology of feather-picking. Research like this should encourage bird owners and veterinarians alike who have long been frustrated by the discouraging work of curing a feather-picker.

AGGRESSIVENESS AND BITING

Initially you may find that your new bird tries to bite whenever you come near. There is nothing abnormal about this sort of behaviour; the bird is still wild and will gradually become tame through training. But it is abnormal for a once tame bird to suddenly change its personality and become openly aggressive. A sudden change like this can usually be traced to some instability in the bird's environment or routine. For instance, inadequate sleep will certainly make a bird restless and irritable. A bird's personality can also be altered by fear, by a bad experience with someone or something, which makes the bird turn on its owner.

Some birds may become resentful over something you have done and decide to "take it out" on you. If you make the mistake of actually hitting the bird, it will certainly turn against you. In fact, any attempt to physically discipline your bird will run the risk of alienating its feelings, so that it no

A bad experience can make a bird turn on its owner.

longer feels safe in your hands. Having lost the bird's trust, you will undoubtedly get nipped the next time you try to handle it.

Don't Be Alarmed – It's Normal

Sometimes courtship behaviour is mistaken for aggressiveness. For instance, a bird may exhibit a "display" behaviour where the head bobs, the tail fans out, and the bird may squat while vibrating its partially opened wings.

A courting bird may pace back and forth quickly on its perch; these actions may also be a warning to stay out of its territory.

Even very tame birds may bite if fingers are poked at them through the cage bars.

A bird's hostility toward some individual does not necessarily mean this person has mistreated the bird. Birds are quite capable of forming personal likes and dislikes. Parrots and other large psittacines are especially inclined to make their "people preferences" known, and their lack of affection for someone may be based on nothing more than the person's sex.

MASTURBATION

Masturbation is generally not considered abnormal behaviour in birds, unless it is done to excess. Nor is it an activity that you should be embarrassed about.

Birds that are caged by themselves and not allowed to mix with their own kind will often turn to masturbation as a sexual outlet. The object of their affection could be a mirror (mistaking the image for a mate), a favourite toy, a rag, a pillow or even some part of their owner's body such as a finger, hand or shoulder. They will rub their vent areas on this object and actually release semen, which you may observe as white drops on the mirror.

If this activity offends you for any reason, the way to stop the bird is to remove the object of his affection, or get him a mate.

Excessive masturbation (the bird does it many times a day, for weeks on end) is considered to be abnormal or neurotic behaviour, and must be classed as a psychological disorder. At present, it is not understood what causes this change in birds; for instance, examinations indicate no diagnostic change in their sex glands. It is also very difficult to stop. Hormonal treatment by a veterinarian may help in some cases.

THE COMPULSIVE FEEDER

Some birds develop a neurotic compulsion to eat and regurgitate. They usually do so in front of a mirror or some other shiny object in which they can see their reflection. Occasionally a bird will do this so often that it gradually loses weight and begins to decline in health because it is not retaining enough food to support itself. These birds should be given a mate, and the mirrors or shiny objects removed from the cage.

CHRONIC EGG-LAYERS

Continuous or prolonged egg-laying is considered a neurosis because it can be triggered by an owner removing eggs from the nest. There are probably some hormonal influences acting on the problem as well. On occasion such a bird will literally "lay" itself to death, producing so many eggs that it becomes physically depleted. Hormonal therapy by a veterinarian may stop some of these chronic egg layers.

DEVOICING

It is surgically possible to "debark" a dog or "demeaow" a cat through a procedure that modifies the vocal cords to reduce the loudness of the sounds made by these animals. However, it is very difficult to "devoice" pet birds in order to mute the harshness or loudness of their voices. A bird's vocal cords are not positioned in the upper throat, as they are in mammals, but are deeper inside the area where the windpipe enters the chest cavity, at the "V" of the clavicle. As a result, devoicing surgery can cause severe damage, and even kill the bird. It is a procedure that should only be considered for peacocks and large roosters.

The bird that squawks or screams a great deal may simply be expressing what is native to his personality and his species. Then again, his screams could be a reaction to boredom or to some condition within his environment – a dirty cage, stale water or a monotonous diet – that he loudly objects to.

A parrot winding up for a good screech.

Your behaviour towards the bird can generate a screeching personality, if you are not careful. Try never to yell at your bird; he may take to shrieking back, or become an even worse screamer. Neither should you tease or frighten your bird, unless you are prepared to live with his raucous scolding.

When your bird screams do not run to him right away. You will simply reinforce his screeching by giving him the attention he craves. The best remedy is to ignore his screams. If he continues, and you simply cannot stand it, put the bird in his cage and cover it, or leave him in the dark. The bird should recognize this as a form of chastisement.

If you have already stretched your ingenuity to the limit looking for a means to silence your "screamer", take heart. There is a way to save your eardrums, and those of your neighbours, without throttling your bird. I refer my reader to an article on "The Squawking Bird," found in Part II of this volume.

7
Befriending Your Bird

When you are buying a pet bird, you will undoubtedly want a tame bird that you can handle. You will enjoy your pet much more if it is responsive to your attentions, well-behaved, and eager to be with you, sitting on your hand or shoulder. But birds like this do not grow on trees – they must be trained. Taming the bird is, of course, your responsibility. It is a procedure that may summon all of your patience, yet the rewards are great, and lasting.

The first step in your procedure is to select a young bird because the young are more receptive to learning. Ask your veterinarian to clip the feathers on one wing because this will make the bird more dependent on you during the taming period. At the same time, have the nails und beak trimmed to save a little wear and tear on your skin. You have to expect a few bites while you are taming birds, particularly with the bigger species, but take these in your stride and try not to overreact.

Leave your bird alone for a week or two until it grows accustomed to its new environment, and locate its cage where the bird will be exposed to a fair amount of household traffic. This will help it get used to the sounds and sight of people. When you see that the bird has settled down, and is becoming more comfortable in its new home, you can begin the taming and training.

Birds can bite very hard. If you are afraid of being bitten, especially by a bad-tempered bird, it is a good idea to protect yourself with some heavy clothing. Wear heavy leather gloves at first, but get rid of these as soon as possible because they may frighten the bird, and make it more aggressive.

The bird should be taken away from its cage while you are trying to tame it. The actual removal of the bird presents no problem if the cage has a large door. If it does not, the bird can sometimes be coaxed onto a wooden perch, or he may voluntarily climb onto your gloved hand. Offer your hand to the bird palm down, fingers together. If you offer just one finger to a big bird, he will bite it until he learns to trust you.

Spend as much time as possible with your bird until it gradually becomes accustomed to having your hands nearby. Teach it to come to you for food. This is best accomplished by keeping your bird a little hungry rather than overfed[1]. Give it seed, morning and evening, and coax it to take the food from you. Eventually you will have the bird eating out of your hand. When

1. See Part II, "Gang Taming," p. 146 in this volume. The article describes the group sessions which familiarize wild birds with the human touch by offering them titbits of food.

this stage is reached, you can begin to touch parts of its body. Most birds will respond to scratching around the head, chest, under the wings and stroking along the back. Be gentle, slow and patient, and you will soon be able to handle your bird without fear of being bitten.

The great challenge and reward of taming is to win your bird's trust. Always move slowly and deliberately. Plan your moves ahead in order not to frighten the bird. If the bird bites at you, restrain your natural reflex to jerk your hand away. Move a short distance out of his reach, just fast enough to prevent the bite, but not to scare him. You can often stop the bird from biting one hand by attracting his attention with the other.

Initially, you may have to wear protective gloves when training your bird.

If the bird gets a good grip on one of your hands, pry its mouth open gently with the other. If the bird makes you angry, put him back in his cage and work with him later when you have calmed down.

Patience and repetition are the two key elements used in training birds. Talk continually to the bird in a soothing voice and this will help ease its apprehension. Remember that you must gain the bird's trust.

TOWEL METHOD

This is a very sensible method for taming big birds.[2] Drape a towel over the back of the bird and wrap it up, leaving only its head exposed; be careful not to damage the feathers. As you are working with the bird, talk to it in a soothing voice all the while. Begin to gently scratch and rub the area around its head and neck. Gradually it will stop squawking and begin to show signs of actually liking the experience. It will remain nervous, but if you persist the bird will start turning its head in various ways to have you scratch different areas.

2. See Part II, "Taming Parrots: Question and Answers," p. 149 in this volume. The article suggests various ways to tame and befriend pet parrots.

Once the bird accepts this procedure and learns that being wrapped in a towel means having its head and neck scratched in a pleasurable way, it will begin to enjoy what you are doing. The next step is to lift the bird up slowly and sit its feet on your hand or arm; let it stand there with the towel still on. Slowly remove the towel and the bird may stay there. If it jumps off, wrap the bird up in the towel once more, then calm it down with the scratching of the head routine and try again.

The final step is reached when the bird consents to remain on your arm, and allows you to scratch its head and body. Some people claim they can tame birds in this manner in a matter of hours.

Handle your bird gently, talk soothingly, be patient, and you will earn your bird's trust.

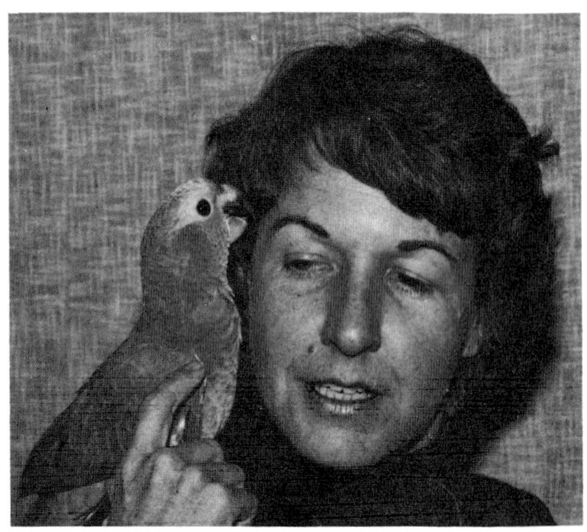

The rewards of proper training: your bird becomes a friend.

TAMING YOUNG AND SMALLER SPECIES

Young birds, especially smaller species like budgies, are best worked on as soon as you get them. Birds raised in captivity are not subjected to the stresses that captured wild birds are, nor do they require the same acclimatization as wild birds.

Wing clipping is recommended because once the bird realizes it cannot fly away from you it will be easier to tame.

Take the bird out of the cage, and let it get used to sitting on your fingers and hand. It can be coaxed onto a finger by gently nudging its chest. When it starts to lose its balance, it will step onto your finger. Try not to pick the bird up bodily too often because this may encourage it to bite.

Once the bird is willing to sit on your fingers, you can easily transfer it to your shoulder. As it loses its fear and learns to trust you, it will become more comfortable with the handling you are giving it.

TEACHING BIRDS TO TALK

A talking bird is simply one that is able to mimic what it hears. There are several methods used to teach birds to talk, including the covered cage technique and training records. But no matter which of these methods is tried, the owner/trainer should first of all tame the bird. It must learn to trust you and feel comfortable in your presence before it will actually start to talk.

Some species pick up talking much more easily than others, and even among these favoured species there will be individual birds that never catch on to the trick of it. Budgies, mynah birds, and parrots like the African Grey, Yellow Naped Amazon, Double Yellow Headed Amazon and the

Macaws learn to talk with ease, and speak in quite a soft voice.

Panama are reputed to be splendid talkers. In some species, however, the males will prove better talkers than the females.

You will be far more pleased with the result if you initially teach your bird to talk rather than whistle. Birds pick up whistling quickly, will probably prefer it to talking and you may find their shrill, ear-piercing blasts are rather hard on the nerves.

If you want your bird to have a large vocabulary, you must be prepared to spend a lot of time with him. The more work you put into his lessons, the greater your satisfaction will be with his achievement.

CAGE COVERING METHOD

This method for training "talkers" was developed in Africa where parrots are common household pets.

Once a day, place your bird in a completely empty cage. Cover the cage with a cloth, and then for a period of about ten minutes talk to the bird. Repeat over and over the simple words you want the bird to say. Keep the words short, and start with just one or two. The strategy of this method is to capture the bird's undivided attention; for a brief period of time he will concentrate on the sound of your voice. Limit the time to ten minutes because a bird's attention span is relatively short. After the lesson, put the bird back in his regular cage.

If you repeat this daily, your bird could begin to talk within a week. As the bird gradually starts to repeat single words, keep reinforcing these through constant repetition. Over a period of time, the bird itself will pick up other words or sounds it frequently hears in its surroundings.

TRAINING RECORDS

There are phonograph records available that are designed to teach birds to talk. These records often shorten the time it takes a bird to learn its first words. Play one side at a time, and repeat the same words yourself to reinforce them in the bird's mind.

The best recording will repeat words slowly and concisely, and it will be more effective if spoken in a female voice. Once the bird shows signs of retaining these words, you can move on to another record. Plan at least one or more 10 to 20 minute learning sessions a day, and it is preferable to hold these at the same time each day.

TONGUE SPLITTING

There is an old wives' tale which contends that a bird must have its tongue split before it can talk. This barbaric practice will not improve the talking ability of any bird; in fact, it may decrease a bird's ability to talk. Under no

1 Budgerigars

2 Canary

3 Purple Grenadier Waxbill

4 African Grey Parrot

5 *Mexican Double Yellow-headed Amazon Parrot*

6 *Fischer's Lovebird*

7 (opposite above) *Jenday Conure*

8 (below left) *Ring-necked Parrakeet*

9 (above) *Blue and Gold Macaws*

10 (right) *Sulphur-crested Cockatoo*

11 Grey Cockatiel (left) *and Lutino Cockatiel*

12 Goldie's Lorikeet

13 Indian Hill Mynah

14 Toco Toucan

15 Domestic Pigeon

16 Male Chinese Painted Quail

circumstances should any bird owner allow this to be done to a bird, regardless of its species.

TALKING TIPS

A young, well-tamed, human oriented bird will learn to talk more easily than an older, untamed bird.

Keep mirrors out of your bird's cage until it learns to talk, otherwise it may jabber away in "bird talk" at its own image.

Once a bird learns to talk well, it rarely forgets.

8
Birds! Birds! Birds!

BUDGERIGAR (plate 1)

SPECIES — *Melopsittacus undulatus* (Family Psittacidae)[1].

ORIGIN — native to drier parts of Australia.

COLOUR **Mature:** – the wild type is basically green with darker barring on the back, wings and head.
- domestic shows infinite combinations of basic shades: green, violet, yellow, blue, white, brown and black.
- upper parts are usually barred with black and yellow or black and white.
- iris of eye is white.
- legs are greyish-blue.

Immature: – do not have the sheen, or distinct colour of the adult; eyes completely dark.
- black spots on throat are ill-defined or absent.
- adult plumage is acquired when about 4 months old.

SEXING **Mature:** – sexes look much alike; cere is blue in males, and brown or pink in females.

Immature: – harder to sex.
- dark colour bars on the forehead, which start close to the cere; they recede to top of head in maturity.
- males have a pink cere; females, a pale blue almost to white.

WEIGHT — average 30–35 gm.

SIZE — average 19 cm (7½ in.) in length, and have long tails.

LIFE SPAN — 6 to 8 years; sometimes reaching 20 years.

DIET — see p. 126.
iodine is a necessary supplement that must be added to the diet.

BREEDING — gregarious birds that breed best if several pairs are kept within sight and sound of each other.
— will breed several times a year (but should be restricted to two broods per year).
— remove and clean the nests after each breeding season.

SEASON — usually early spring, but most will breed any time of year.

---

1. This family numbers over 300 species, including green parrots, African Greys, Macaws, Love Birds, Parrakeets and Budgies.

BROOD SIZE — 3–6 white eggs will hatch in an average of 18 days, brood leaves the nest at 4–5 weeks of age.

NEST TYPE — a nest box, homemade or purchased, is attached to the side of the cage.

CAGE TYPE — cage must be designed for budgies, not canaries. Budgie cage has bars that are parallel and do not taper.
— rectangular metal cage; minimum size of 2 cubic feet, 1' × 1' × 2'.

Budgies are the most popular cage bird. The reason for their popularity is their affectionate nature and their adeptness at talking. With very little effort and training, these birds build up an extensive vocabulary.

When buying a budgie, choose a lively bird that is alert and not easily frightened. And try to select a young one. An immature budgie will be tamed more easily, and can learn to talk. An adult is unlikely to do so. Male birds seem to talk better than females, although some people maintain that both sexes talk equally well.

Budgies are free spirits. They enjoy flying about the house, rather than being cooped up in a cage all the time. However, let them first get used to their cage environment before you allow them out of it. Finger training can often be started right in the cage. If you have the wings clipped to prevent flying, you can take them out of the cage within a few days. Once tamed, they become very sociable little companions who will love every bit of attention you can give.

Although budgies moult once a year, they do not lose all their feathers at the same time; the process will go on for several weeks and even months. The moult can occur at any time during the year, and sometimes goes into an inactive period before the moulting and feather regrowth starts again.

Healthy budgies normally sit on one foot when resting or sleeping, so that conversely, a budgie resting on two feet may not be well. By nature budgies are quite hardy, but they are subject to a lot of diseases. Feed them well, look after them properly and they should live for many years.

CANARY (Plate 2)

SPECIES — *Serinus canaria* (Family Fringillidae).

ORIGIN — the Canary Islands and various parts of Europe.

COLOUR **Mature:**
- native wild canaries are greenish-yellow with yellow, dark-streaked underparts.
- main domestic colours: yellow, orange, olive, white, brown and black; in infinite combinations.

Immature:
- same colour.
- have a plumper baby face, and no scales on the feet.

SEXING **Mature:** – both sexes look alike, but the following may help:
- the vent of a breeding male is more prominent, and tilts slightly upward when he is held on his back.
- the breeding female's vent becomes enlarged, but does not protrude quite as far as the male's; when placed on her back, the vent lies almost parallel to the body.

Immature: – sexing is difficult.

MOULTING — usually moult from July to October.

WEIGHT — average 20 gm.

SIZE — average 12.5–14 cm (5–5½ in.) in length.

LIFE SPAN — 6–9 years; sometimes reaching 20 years.

DIET — see p. 129.

BREEDING — breed well. Too high a temperature will stop the breeding cycle and start a premature moult.
— provide a quiet environment for nesting birds.
— restrict breeding birds to two nests a year.
— remove and clean the nests after each breeding season.

SEASON — spring, when the wild birds begin to nest.

BROOD SIZE — 3–6 creamy white eggs will hatch in about 14 days.
— brood leaves the nest at about 16 days.

NEST TYPE — require a shallow bowl with nesting material like fine grass placed on the bottom of their cage.

CAGE TYPE — should be metal and rectangular; minimum size of 2 cubic feet, 1' × 1' × 2'.

Canaries are the second most popular cage bird. Over 28 different varieties are bred in captivity. They are good-natured birds, with attractive plumage and beautiful singing voices.

Selective breeding has divided canaries into two sub groups: Song and Type canaries. Song canaries are bred mainly for their voices, while the type canaries are bred for their looks. The song canaries are further divided, in America at least, into "Choppers" and "Rollers". Choppers sing loudly with their beaks wide open, while rollers sing with their beaks nearly closed. The chopper is the more common and least expensive of the two but is available only in America.

If you wish to buy a canary for its singing ability, make sure you actually hear it sing first. Avoid a canary that is moulting because this bird is already under stress, and putting it into a new environment will only heighten its problems. Canaries are out of moult in the winter, spring and early summer; these are the best times to purchase your bird. You will also find that a cheaply priced canary is likely a female. The females do not sing as well as the males, and are priced accordingly. You should also look for a young bird, under two years of age.

Canaries thrive in temperatures of 15° to 21°C (60°–70°F). Higher temperatures may cause premature moulting, which is difficult to stop[2]. They must be kept as cool as possible in the hot summer months, without chilling them.

Canaries prefer to bathe in the morning. During the summer, the bird should be encouraged to bathe every second day; twice a week is sufficient in the winter. Bathing is particularly important for the canary because it helps keep the bird's feet clean. Canaries have a tendency toward foot and leg problems, especially those caused by a build-up of droppings or by accumulated layers of dead skin[3]. The conscientious owner must help the bird keep these areas clean and supple.

FINCH (Plate 3)

FAMILY — Estrildidae.

ORIGIN — found throughout the world.

COLOUR — There are many species of finch, some of which are domesticated and bred in a large number of mutations.

SEXING **Mature:** – sexes look alike in many species; others have characteristic differences (consult a guide to Finches for exact descriptions).

WEIGHT — ranges from 10 to 35 gm on average.

SIZE — from 7.5. to 15 cm (3–6 in.) in length.

LIFE SPAN — approximately 5–8 years.

DIET — see p. 131.

BREEDING — most species will breed in captivity.
— an average pair of birds will raise two broods a year, usually one after the other.
— the nest should be removed after the second brood and cleaned before re-use.
— overbreeding will weaken the offspring and the parents.

SEASON — the majority of species breed in the spring or fall; others breed any time of the year.

BROOD SIZE — averages 3 to 7 per nest.
— incubation averages 12–14 days; the young leave the nest at 2–3 weeks.
— egg colour is not standard for all finches, but the majority are white or cream-coloured.

NEST TYPE — varies with the species, but most like grass or wicker nests,

2. Referred to as a soft moult.
3. See p. 83.

or nest boxes; the latter should be provided along with fine dry grass, commercial nesting material or nesting hair.

CAGE TYPE — do better in large, custom made aviaries, which give them a lot of freedom.
— they like company and should not be housed alone.
— rectangular; minimum cage size of 2 cubic feet, 1' × 1' × 2'.

Finches come in a rainbow of colours and a variety of fascinating personalities. Some do have singing ability, some change colours, during the breeding season and some just remain their beautiful selves.

They are called "hardbill" birds because their main diet is seed, although they do have other food requirements as well.

There are innumerable varieties and species of finch. A few of the more common varieties are mentioned here.

Zebra Finch

Zebras are probably the most common, lowest priced and most easily bred finch. Colour mutations are common and varied. These birds are attractive, active, very friendly and a pleasure to keep. They get along well with other birds. Description: males usually have a large, rusty-coloured cheek patch just below the eye. Fine horizontal bars of black and greyish-white extend from chin to chest; the sides and flanks are chestnut with prominent white spots. The females are rather drab. Both have orange feet, legs and beaks. About 10 cm (4 in.) long.

Society or Bengalese Finch

Runs a close second to the Zebra finch in popularity, and is similarly priced. They are happy, friendly little birds, and get along well with other species. They make good breeders and are quite hardy. Description: sexes are similar in colour, varying from white to dark brown; most are mottled brown and white, or cinnamon and white. Feet, legs and beak are light brown. About 11 cm (4½ in.) long.

Owl Finch

Has a friendly, delightful personality and is quite charming. They are amiable with other birds, and make fairly good breeders. Description: a combination of white, greys and dark brown. A black cap extends around the white face and underneath the neck; the back and tail are dark, and the wings spotted. Another dark band crosses the lower chest, which is also white. The male has wide, bold colour bands and bright white underparts; the female is a duller white. About 9 cm (3½ in.) long.

Diamond Sparrow

Is not a true sparrow. These attractive finches are good breeders. Description: the head, back and wings are dark browny-grey; the throat is white, the breast is black, mottled with white, and there is a large area of red on the rump and tail coverts. The beak and eye ring are also red. The females have a brighter red beak, but are difficult to distinguish from the males. About 12.5 cm (5 in.) long.

Java Sparrows

Are very popular, hardy, readily available and relatively inexpensive. They are not noted for their singing ability, but are very attractive birds and make fairly good breeders. It is best to keep them in large cages or aviaries to save damage to their feathers; they may also bully smaller birds, so are better housed with larger species like the budgies. Description: grey with a black head and neck, and a large white cheek patch. The beak and eye ring are a dark pinkish colour, while the feet and legs are lighter pink. White and pied mutations have been established. About 14 cm (5½ in.) long.

AFRICAN GREY PARROT (Plate 4)

SPECIES — *Psittacus erithacus* (Family Psittacidae).
ORIGIN — native to tropical West and Central Africa.
COLOUR
Mature:
- grey with white face area; tail and adjacent tail coverts are red; legs are dove grey that lightens with age.
- eyes have a pale yellow iris with a dark pupil.

Immature:
- eyes are solid dark grey to black.
- feet are dark-coloured and smooth.
- tail is dark red towards the tip; under tail coverts are grey tinged.

SEXING[4] — Both sexes look alike.
WEIGHT — *400—500 gm.*
SIZE — average 33 cm (13½ in.) in length.
LIFE SPAN — 20–25 years; sometimes reaching 70 years.
DIET — see pp. 136–40.
BREEDING — rare in captivity but becoming more common.
SEASON — usually spring and summer.
BROOD SIZE — 2–4 light-coloured eggs will hatch in 17–31 days.
— brood leaves the nest at 9–10 weeks.

---

4. Some birds can only be readily sexed by a surgical procedure called endoscopy or laparoscopy. A special optical instrument is inserted into the abdominal cavity through a small incision, and the surgeon directly observes the gonads or sex organs of the bird to see whether it has testicles or ovaries.

NEST TYPE — hollow logs, buckets, or converted garbage pails with entrance holes.

CAGE TYPE — rectangular; minimum size of 18–24 cubic feet, 2′× 3′ × 3′/2 ′×3′ × 4′.

This well-known parrot is reputed to be the best talking parrot. It is very intelligent, and has an uncanny ability to mimic the human voice. The African Grey is quite affectionate, and, once tamed, it readily accepts being handled, and often develops lasting friendships with other family pets. The bird will give its owner many hours of enjoyment with the variety of noises it makes, the vocabulary it can pick up, and the antics it performs.

Although it does require persistence and patience, taming is usually achieved eventually, and the end result is well worth the effort put into the bird. Not all greys learn to talk, but the majority are good achievers. An older, wild bird is rather difficult to tame, so it is preferable to purchase a young, outgoing bird.

In general, members of the parrot family are easily recognized by their large hooked beak, which often doubles as an extra foot when the birds are climbing about. Their feet have two toes pointing forward and two toes pointing backward, enabling them to use their feet like hands when grasping and holding food.

Parrots are from the warm climes, and consequently the temperature of their captive environment is an important factor in their well-being. A warm environment, free from draughts, is the ideal. They may be kept outdoors at temperatures colder than 19°C (65°F), providing proper shelter is available to protect them from the wind.

These birds enjoy their freedom and like to be out of the cage as much as possible – where the action is. Being intelligent birds, they can become bored quite easily, especially if neglected by their owner or kept in a cage of insufficient size, and this boredom can result in feather-picking problems. While they are fond of human companionship, they are also discriminating. Many parrots select a favourite person in the household to whom they allow special liberties that are denied to others.

If you are considering buying a parrot, think first about the amount of time you spend away from home. If you have little time for the bird, your better choice would be a less demanding species like the canaries or finches. Parrots also have certain idiosyncrasies you should be aware of.

They enjoy being vocal, and they can wolf whistle at a volume equal to a siren. Once a word is learned, they tend to repeat it for hours until the owner may wish he had never taught the bird to talk. Parrots are more vocal in the morning and evening. If you enjoy peace and quiet, or live where the noise might bother your neighbours, you had best think twice about buying a parrot.

Parrots can also be very messy. They are notorious for flinging food farther than any other species of bird: whatever they do not like, they either drop or pitch aside. After eating sticky fruits, they wipe their beaks on whatever is handy: the cage, the perch, or even you. Their short digestive tract also means that they defaecate frequently. Be prepared to have a lot of paper on stand-by.

Like many of the exotic species, parrots do require more of their owners. But in weighing the parrot's idiosyncrasies against its charming, bright personality, many people feel the scale more than tips in favour of the bird. If your heart is set on a parrot, think about the species you want and why you want it: the African Greys along with the Double Yellow Headed parrots, the Macaws and Yellow Napes learn to talk easily; the Amazons, cockatoos and rosellas are the pranksters. Then take the time to select a good one. Consider the bird's age, health and personality when you are finally ready to make your choice.

AMAZON PARROTS

GENUS — *Amazona* (Family Psittacidae).

ORIGIN — range from South and Central America to northern Mexico.

COLOUR
- **Mature:** – predominant colour is green with areas of yellow, orange, white or blue on the head, wings or tail.
- **Immature:** – are less colourful; have no scars on feet or face.
  - – make grunting or hissing noises.
  - – show no growth ridges on beak or nails.
  - – legs are smooth up to 2 years; beyond that they become rough, scaly and calloused.

SEXING — no visible distinguishing features between the sexes.

WEIGHT — medium parrots about 300 gm; larger parrots about 450–500 gm.

SIZE — from 24 to 52.5 cm (9½–21 in.) in length.

LIFE SPAN — 30–70 years.

DIET — see pp. 136–40.

BREEDING — large environment with adequate nesting facilities must be created for these birds to breed and raise young.
— some breeding birds may become bad-tempered and protective of the nest during the breeding season.

SEASON — early spring to mid-summer.

BROOD SIZE — 2–5 white or creamy white eggs will hatch in 26–28 days.
— brood leaves the nest at 8–10 weeks.

NEST TYPE — hollow trees, wooden barrels or large nest boxes.

CAGE TYPE — requires lots of exercise room.
— rectangular; minimum size of 18 cubic feet, 2′ × 3′ × 4′, depending on size of bird.

The Amazon is the commonest pet parrot in Canada and the USA. There are approximately 30 different Amazon species. Some of these become very accomplished talking birds and most make good pets, especially if acquired young. They were named after the Amazon river in South America where the species were first found by early explorers.

These are a few of the more common species:

Yellow-Naped Amazon
Have the nicest nature, and are among the best talking Amazons. The bird is quite hardy and very easily trained. Description: basically green with a yellow band across the back of the neck, a patch of red on each wing and a bluish shade on the wing tips.

Mexican Double Yellow-Headed Amazon (Plate 5)
A very popular bird in North America, generally regarded as an excellent talker with an affectionate personality. This is not always the case. Some have exhibited nasty personalities, and even a few of the excellent talkers can be aggressive. Description: basically green with a yellow head and neck (the older the bird, the larger this area of yellow), and yellow on the tip of the tail. The shoulders are splashed with red, yellow and a touch of blue.

Yellow-Fronted Amazon
Its talking ability is excellent, and it usually has quite a friendly personality. Description: basically green with a patch of yellow extending from the forehead into the crown; the shoulders and secondary wing feathers are splashed with red.

Green-Cheeked Amazon
Sometimes called Mexican Red Head Amazons, they are fairly affectionate and can become quite good talkers. Description: basically green with a red cap on the crown, bright green cheeks, a touch of lavender above the eye and back of the head, and a patch of red and blue on each wing.

Orange-Winged Amazon
Very affectionate birds that become moderately good talkers. Description: basically green with a yellow forehead and cheek patch, and a violet-blue band above the eyes; a green, yellow and orange tail, and orangey-red wing patches.

LOVE BIRDS

GENUS — *Agapornis* (Family Psittacidae).
ORIGIN — Africa
COLOUR **Mature:** – predominantly green with orange, yellow, blue, black, white or grey markings.
– usually more brightly coloured on head, neck and rump.
Immature: – similar to adults.
SEXING — no external differences.
WEIGHT — 45–60 gm.
SIZE — 13–15 cm (4½–6 in.) in length.
LIFE SPAN — 10–14 years.
DIET — see p. 139.
BREEDING — some species, such as Peach-faced and Masked, breed easily in captivity, once provided with proper nesting material.
— will interbreed with different species.
SEASON — year round.
BROOD SIZE — 3–7 whitish eggs, usually laid twice a year; will hatch in 18–24 days.
— brood leaves the nest at 5–6 weeks.
NEST TYPE — requires nest box lined with small pieces of bark, grass or leaves.
CAGE TYPE — rectangular; minimum size of 12 cubic feet, 2′× 2′ × 3′.

Love Birds are intelligent, curious creatures, with quite aggressive personalities. Older wild birds are difficult to tame, but the young or hand-raised birds turn into very affectionate pets that will follow you around the house if allowed their freedom. They often take to one person in the household, and may even show their preference by ignoring everyone else. Some will also learn to talk if you are persistent enough in their training.

Love Birds acquired their name from their co-operative habit of preening each other. They have small, stocky builds and are quite aggressive with other species, yet highly compatible among themselves. In fact, two birds of the same sex will often set up housekeeping. Few "pairs" are actually male and female, even though the owners of these birds are convinced that they have a true pair. This "same sex" pair live quite happily and go through all the antics of making a nest – the females will even lay sterile eggs.

They are busy birds and great little chewers, so appropriate chewing material must be provided. Unless given an interesting environment and a variety of things to play with, Love Birds have a tendency to become feather-pickers and may even pluck out each other's feathers. They are certainly hardy enough to do well in an outdoor aviary, if given good nest boxes to sleep in.

Of the nine species of Love Birds, these are the types people often choose for pets:

Peach-Faced Love Bird
The commonest, largest and most pugnacious of the Love Birds, yet the type most often chosen as a pet. Description: a pastel green colour with a rose-coloured face and neck; the upper tail coverts are blue.

Masked Love Bird
Second only in popularity to the Peach-Faced, the Masked is quieter, less pugnacious and has a pleasant personality. Description: bright green wings and abdomen; black head with red beak, white eye rings, and a yellowish collar and chest.

There is a blue mutation as well. Description: black head with light pink beak; blue on the wings and abdomen, and a whitish collar and chest.

CONURES

FAMILY	— Psittacidae.	
ORIGIN	— found throughout southern Mexico, Central and South America.	
COLOUR	**Mature:**	– a wide range of colour combinations of red, orange, yellow, blue, brown, white and black, with green being the predominant body colour.
	Immature:	– similar to adults.
SEXING	**Mature:**	– no external differences between sexes of most species.
WEIGHT	— 70–150 gm.	
SIZE	— 22–45 cm (9–18 in.) in length.	
LIFE SPAN	— 8–15 years.	
DIET	— see p. 136.	
BREEDING	— several species are being bred in captivity.	
SEASON	— early spring and summer.	
BROOD SIZE	— 2–5 on average, but some species will lay up to 7 eggs; will hatch in 23–25 days.	
	— brood leaves the next at approximately 8 weeks.	
NEST TYPE	— artificial nest boxes.	
CAGE TYPE	— large, rectangular; a minimum size of 12 cubic feet, 2′ × 2′ × 3′.	

Conures are very similar in shape and appearance to Macaws, though generally much smaller. They have long slender bodies with a long tapering tail. Of the 50 or more species and subspecies, only a few are kept as pets.

Generally, they are not easy to tame unless acquired very young. Tame conures can be as affectionate as a budgie, and will talk reasonably well if a lot of effort is put into teaching them. People who have made this effort find that conures are very enjoyable pets.

Invariably, the conures that you see in aviaries are the more colourful varieties. Those most frequently seen include:

Jenday Conure (Plate 7)
Colour is this bird's main asset because it has a loud, raucous voice. Some have been tamed and taught to talk, but most are never trained. One of the favourite types because it breeds freely in captivity but difficult to obtain since legal export from its country of origin, Brazil, was stopped. Description: yellow head, neck and chest; green back and wings; deep red abdomen; bluish wing tips with the upper tail being greenish, shading to bluish-black at the tip. The male is about 25 cm (10 in.) long.

Halfmoon Conure or Petz' Conure
A very popular pet that is often sold as a "dwarf parrot". If you buy one, be sure it is young or already tamed; an untamed adult is hard to deal with. A tamed Halfmoon makes a very delightful pet, and young birds are fairly easily tamed. Description: basically green in colour, and lighter on the underparts; a bluish tinge to the wing-flight feathers; yellowish eye ring, and an orange forehead. There is a blue colour on the crown of the head. About 24 cm (9½ in.) long.

Nanday Conure
Can be quite noisy, but if tamed when very young, they tend to be quieter and can be made into a delightful pet. It is not a very good talker, and is quite fond of chewing. Description: the back, neck, wing and tail are a bright green; the head and beak are black, the wing-flight feathers a bluish-black, the chest is tinged with blue and the abdomen, with light orange. The thighs are bright red. About 25 cm (10 in.) long.

PARRAKEETS (INCLUDES ROSELLAS)

FAMILY — Psittacidae.
ORIGIN — Africa, Australia, China, New Guinea, Ceylon and India.
COLOUR **Mature:**
- are predominantly green; a number of the larger species have a band of colour around the throat and neck.
- the smaller species come in a wide range of colour combinations; green is the dominant colour.
- rosellas are more brightly coloured birds

		in basic shades of red, orange, yellow, green, blue and black; all have cheek patches and fairly long tails.
	Immature:	– colour differences do occur, but vary with the species.
SEXING	**Mature:**	– most species are not sexually dimorphic.
	Immature:	– same as adult.

WEIGHT — 60–200 gm.

SIZE — small parrakeets: 14–28 cm (5½–11 in.); large parrakeets: 30–40 cm (12–16 in.); rosellas; 25–36 cm (10–15 in).

LIFE SPAN — 10–15 years

DIET — see p. 139.

BREEDING — many are being bred successfully in captivity.

SEASON — early spring to late summer.

BROOD SIZE — small parrakeets: 2–7 eggs, will hatch in 18–21 days; brood leaves the nest at 6–8 weeks.
— large parrakeets: 2–4 eggs, will hatch in 21–28 days; brood leaves nest at 6–8 weeks.
— rosellas: 5–7 eggs, will hatch in 18–21 days; brood leaves nest at 6–8 weeks.

NEST TYPE — standard nest box is sufficient.

CAGE TYPE — rectangular; minimum size of 12–18 cubic feet, 2′ × 2′ × 3′, depending on size of bird.

These beautiful birds are starting to become very popular with aviculturists. There are many species and subspecies, including the whole rosella family group, but only a few of these are found in captivity.

The smaller species, especially the various Australian Grass Parrakeets are not recommended as house pets. They need the more specialized care that is better provided in an aviary by an aviculturist. However, the larger species can certainly be kept as pets though they are difficult birds to tame, and are not generally known as talking birds. Usually they are kept for their beautiful colours.

These are three of the commonest. They are species parrakeets you will likely see and be able to obtain:

Indian Ringneck Parrakeet (Plate 8)
One of the larger, more common species, and also one of the loveliest. They breed quite easily in captivity, and get along well with other species in an aviary. They can be tamed, but are not generally known as talkers. They do, however, have pleasant, quiet personalities. Description: a pretty pastel green that lightens on the underparts. The beak is reddish; the male has a fine black line extending from the base of the lower beak to the back of the neck; a pale blue and rose ring borders the black. The primary wing feathers

are tinged with blue on top and a yellowish green underneath. The females and immatures are a duller colour with the rings of colour being absent on the neck. It may take two or three years before the colour difference becomes apparent. The males are about 40 cm (15 in.) long.

Red-rump Parrakeet
Also very pretty birds, having a pleasant, melodious whistle. They are pugnacious with smaller psittacine birds, and are best kept on their own. They are not a talking species. Description: the back is a browny green with a turquoise-green patch on each wing; the head is also green, and the lower chest and abdomen are yellow. Males have a red patch on the rump (the females do not), and the beak is small and dark. The female's head is not as brightly coloured, and the immatures are a duller version of both sexes. About 27 cm (10½ in.) long.

Crimson Rosella
Are popular aviary birds with nice personalities. They do not talk. They are mostly kept in aviaries for breeding purposes because of their colour. Description: the entire head, neck, rump and lower parts are a beautiful crimson red while the cheek patches are blue. The tail is pale blue underneath, and dark blue and green on top; the upper wing coverts are a pale violet-blue. Both sexes are similar in colour. About 33 cm (13 in.) long.

MACAWS

FAMILY — Psittacidae.
ORIGIN — found in Mexico, Central and South America as far south as Paraguay and southern Brazil.
COLOUR **Mature:** – come in a rainbow of colour combinations: basic shades of green, yellow, orange, blue, red, and rusty brown.
Immature: – similar to adults.
SEXING **Mature:** – difficult; few external differences.
Immature: – similar to adults.
WEIGHT — wide variation; 300–1200 gm.
SIZE — 30–100 cm (12–40 in.) in length.
LIFE SPAN — up to 60 years or more.
DIET — see p.136.
BREEDING — Macaws nest readily in captivity and are often prolific.
SEASON — early spring and summer.
BROOD SIZE — 2–5 white eggs; will hatch in 23–28 days.
— brood leaves the nest at 3 months.
NEST TYPE — hollow trees, wooden barrels or nest boxes.

CAGE TYPE — large birds (80 cm/30 in.) rectangular cages; minimum size of 32 cubic feet, 2′ × 4′ × 4′.
— Small birds (30–50 cm/12–20 in.) rectangular cages; minimum size of 18 cubic feet, 2′ × 3′ × 3′.

Macaws are the largest members of the parrot family, of which there are 30 species and subspecies. These handsome long-tailed birds are very colourful, and very hardy. Their intelligence and sense of humour merge in a delightful way to produce a playful, inquisitive nature. The untutored voice of a macaw is loud and harsh, but when it talks, the voice becomes quite soft. The birds learn to talk with ease, and can also be taught to do tricks and acrobatics, which they perform with evident enjoyment.

If you are interested in purchasing a macaw, you should know a few basic facts about its ownership. The macaw is a large bird that will require a lot of time, attention, and room – both in its cage and greater environment. If the bird's activity is restrained by too small a cage or infrequent exercise, it could develop psychological disorders that are hard on the bird's health and worrisome to you. In the interest of the bird's welfare, it should also be supplied with enough chewing materials to satisfy it.

Many macaws are very loving and affectionate, but a few can be vicious. The bite from such a bird can mean the loss of a finger, so do be careful. Never let small children play with a macaw, regardless of the bird's personality. The bird should have only one handler: the person who looks after it all the time.

These are the macaws people often choose as pets:

Blue and Gold Macaw (Plate 9)
One of the more intelligent and better talking macaws, but quite mischievous. Description: underparts from the neck to tail are yellow-gold; the crown, neck, back and tail are a rich blue. The cheeks are bare, the forehead green, the bib black. One of the larger macaws, 85–90 cm (34–36 in.) long.

Scarlet Macaw
These birds are friendly, quite intelligent and fairly good talkers. Description: brilliant red except for the wings, base of the tail and its underparts, which are dark blue; the wings below the shoulder are yellow with tinges of green. The cheeks are decorated with fine rows of inconspicuous red feathers. About 85–90 cm (34–36 in.) long.

Green-Winged Macaw
They are friendly birds and demonstrate a fairly good talking ability. Description: similar to the Scarlet except for the green and blue on their wings. The cheeks are bare but traversed by lines of red feathers. About 85–90 cm (34–36 in.) long.

Hyacinth Macaw
Quite expensive birds because they are rarer than the other large species. They are rather boisterous, with good personalities, but limited talking ability. Description: an overall cobalt blue with a yellow eye ring, and a yellow bare area at the base of the lower beak. The cheeks are feathered. The largest macaw, about 100 cm (40 in.) long.

Military Macaw
These birds are easily tamed, have pleasant personalities and are moderately good talkers. Description: an overall green with a slight olive tinge on its back and wings; bluish tinge colours the back of the neck, and the forehead is red. The cheeks are bare. About 70 cm (27 in.) long.

Severe Macaw
Also called the Chestnut-Fronted Macaw, it is probably the most popular and easily obtained of the dwarf macaws, and is quite a capable talker. It may prove noisy, but overall it is an excellent pet with a gentle nature. Description: basically green with chestnut brown on the forehead, chin, and borders of the bare cheek areas. The tail's underside is browny-red, and the inner parts of the shoulders are red. One of the dwarf macaws, about 50 cm (20 in.) long.

COCKATOOS

FAMILY — Cacatuidae.
ORIGIN — native to Australia, the South Pacific and the Phillipines.
COLOUR
Mature:
- main colour is white, with pink, orange or yellow. A few species are black or greyish.
- legs usually dark grey.

Immature:
- similar to adults.

SEXING
Mature:
- few external differences.
- females of some species have a reddish-brown eye colour.
- eye colour of males remains dark brown or almost black; adult males usually have larger head and bill than females.

Immature:
- no reliable differences.

WEIGHT — 300–800 gm.
SIZE — varies with the different species 31–67 cm (12–27 in.) in length.
LIFE SPAN — 25–45 years; some have even reached 100 years.
DIET — see pp. 136.
BREEDING — quite often bred in captivity.

SEASON	— spring and summer.
BROOD SIZE	— 1–3 white eggs, except Roseate Cockatoo which may lay 5 or 6; will hatch in 25–32 days.
	— brood leaves the nest 10–14 weeks after hatching, except Roseate Cockatoo (8 weeks).
NEST TYPE	— hollow trees, wooden barrels or nest boxes.
CAGE TYPE	— like all members of the parrot family, cockatoos have very strong beaks, and so, require sturdy cages.
	— short pieces of tree branch (with the bark left on) should be available in the cage for chewing.
	— rectangular; minimum size of 24 cubic feet, 2′ × 3′ × 4′.

Cockatoos are very affectionate, anxious to please and quite devoted to their owners. They thrive in captivity and seem to enjoy human companionship. Some do learn to talk, but in the main, they are kept for their intelligence, beauty and ability to learn tricks.

These birds have spectacular crests, which they raise immediately upon alighting after flight, or when alarmed and excited. They also give off a peculiar hissing sound when frightened or alarmed. The hissing noise is usually issued as a warning, whereas the screech they sometimes come out with – a harsh, penetrating blast – can mean anything from joy to outrage.

Cockatoos produce a lot of feather dust or powder, which helps to clean and lubricate their feathers, and maintain their brilliant colours. Chewing is one of their favourite pastimes, and to satisfy this urge they need a steady supply of wood and tree branches.

These are the cockatoos people usually choose as pets:

Roseate or Rose-Breasted Cockatoo

Also called Galah cockatoo, it is a good domestic breeder. These birds are very affectionate and make reasonably good talkers. Description: light pink on the chest and upper half of head, and dark pink from the head's lower half down to the chest and abdomen; grey on wings, tail and back. The iris is dark brown in males, pink-red in females. About 35 cm (15 in.) long.

Greater Sulphur-Crested Cockatoo (Plate 10)

One of the larger, better known and very popular species. It has a very lovable nature, and can be taught to talk. Description: white with yellow on the crest and the undersides of the wings and tail. The iris is dark brown in males, dark, brown to reddish-brown in females. About 50 cm (20 in.) long.

Lesser Sulphur-Crested Cockatoo

Similar in appearance to the Greater, but much smaller. Also very lovable and fairly popular, but not a good talker. About 33 cm (13 in.) long.

Leadbeater's Cockatoo

Also called the Major Mitchell's Cockatoo, it is very affectionate and a moderate talker. Description: white with a beautiful salmon-pink colour blended into the upper part of body, head and chest; a band of darker pink crosses the crest. The iris is dark brown in males, reddish-pink in females. About 35 cm (15 in.) long.

COCKATIELS

SPECIES	— *Nymphicus hollandicus* (Family Cacatuidae).	
ORIGIN	— Australia.	
COLOUR	**Mature:**	– basic body colours: grey, yellow, white and silvery light brown, though variations of each are found; all have the distinctive face and head colourings.
	Immature:	– same as females.
SEXING	**Mature:**	– easy to differentiate in the Grey. – males have a bright yellow face with yellow extending into the crest, and a brilliant orange spot on each cheek. – underside of the tail is dark grey. – a male develops adult plumage at the first moult which may take up to its first year to complete. – females have a slight yellow tinge on the face and crest; cheek patches a much duller orange. The under surface of their wings often have yellow spots; the undersides of their tails have irregular horizontal bars of grey and yellow.
	Immature:	– same colouring as adult females. – wing spots and tail bars are usually visible on the female by 6 months of age.
WEIGHT	— 80–90 gm.	
SIZE	— 32 cm (12½ in.) in length.	
LIFE SPAN	— 10–14 years, but known to live up to 30 years.	
DIET	— see pp. 136–40.	
BREEDING	— require a large cage, lots of exercise, large nest box and privacy. — usually do not start until they are 1–1½ years old; restrict them to two broods a year. — remove and clean the nest after each breeding season, or the parents will start another family.	
SEASON	— will breed at any time of the year.	

BROOD SIZE — 4–8 white eggs, will hatch in 18–20 days.
require bathing water to keep their eggs moist.
— brood leaves the nest at 5 weeks.

NEST TYPE — a nest box, large enough for both birds to enter.
— should be 25 cm (10 in.) square and about 45 cm (18 in.) high, with a 8.8–9.5 cm (3½–3¾ in.) entrance hole. Use wood shavings as a nesting material.

CAGE TYPE — large, roomy, rectangular cages are best.
— minimum cage size of 12 cubic feet, 2′× 2′× 2′ × 3′.

Cockatiels are very popular pets. They are hardy, easily tamed, and learn to both talk and whistle. Some have even learned to do tricks. Most have a good disposition and become very affectionate, lovable pets. A mischievous nature makes them eternally curious, and they always want to investigate their environment. They get along well with other birds, and can be kept in large aviaries with a variety of small species. Often they become quite attached to budgies. They should not, however, be caged with large parrots, or they could be injured.

Young birds are always easier to tame because they become familiar with things more quickly. Sometimes even the older birds can be tamed and then taught to speak, if you persist and have the patience. Both sexes will learn to talk. Tame cockatiels are very affectionate pets.

Some of the lighter-coloured cockatiels, especially the lutinos, have a bald patch on the top of their heads under the crest. This patch varies in size with different birds, and is a normal feature. It is no cause for alarm.

People are inclined to choose their pet cockatiels by colour. Several colours have evolved through selective breeding, the main varieties being:

Grey (Plate 11)
The most common and original colour of the wild birds. Description: grey body with orange cheek patches and dark brown eyes; the males have a yellow face.

Pied
Difficult to sex. Description: some of the grey is replaced by a yellowish colour; varying from off-white to a lemon yellow; the eyes are dark brown.

Lutino (Plate 11)
Similarly difficult to sex; also called albinos, but they are not true albinos. Description: The eyes are red; they have orange cheek patches, and the body is white with some yellow under the wings and tail, and on the body in some birds.

Cinnamon

Description: basically a silvery light brown; the eyes are dark brown and the adult males have a yellow face.

Fallow

Description: like the cinnamon, but the eyes are red.

Pearl

Description: basically grey with dark brown eyes; immature males and adult females have white or yellow spots across the wings and back, and may have a yellow hue in the face and tail area. Mature males look like grey males.

LORIES AND LORIKEETS (Plate 12)

FAMILY — Loriidae.

ORIGIN — found in New Guinea, Australia, Bali and other Indonesian islands, New Hebrides Islands, Solomon Islands, Philippine Islands, Fiji Islands and South Pacific Islands.

COLOUR **Mature:** – basic body colour is green or red, with combination of: orange, blue, black and yellow, white and red.

Immature: – similar to adults.

SEXING **Mature:** – generally difficult; few external differences between sexes.

– some species have colour differences.

WEIGHT — 35–200 gm.

SIZE — 13–42 cm (5–17 in.) in length.

LIFE SPAN — 10–15 years approx.

DIET — see p. 134.

BREEDING — some species are being bred in captivity under controlled conditions.

SEASON — any time of year; some species will choose specific months.

BROOD SIZE — 1–4 eggs, will hatch in 22–25 days.

— brood leaves the nest in 6–11 weeks.

NEST TYPE — nest box should vary in size according to species, from 10 cm (4 in.) square and 25 cm (10 in.) high (or budgie nest box), to 23 cm (9 in.) square and 45 cm (18 in.) high for largest species.

CAGE TYPE — rectangular; minimum size of 18 cubic feet, 2′ × 3′× 3′.

There are 11 genera in this subfamily, which in turn comprises about 50 species. They come in a large assortment of colours from the rather plain to the very beautiful. Although they are not talking birds, they are loved for their beautiful colour and provide many hours of enjoyment for their owner. They are primarily kept in aviaries rather than as pets.

Their diet requirements, however, are rather specialized in that they eat ripe fruits and nectar from flowers. They have a peculiar, brushlike tongue, which enables them to lick up the flower nectar. Before choosing these species as pets, be sure you are willing to meet the specialized demands of their diet.

The droppings of lories and lorikeets are fairly liquid because of the quantities of moisture they digest in their food. This means that the cage will require frequent cleaning. A dutiful owner also supplies these birds with generous amounts of bathing water: bathing is one of their favourite occupations.

Lories and lorikeets adjust well to captivity and have proved to be very robust birds. However, they are better housed separately with their own kind because they tend to gang up on other species and kill them.

INDIAN HILL MYNAH (Plate 13)

SPECIES — *Gracula religiosa* (Family Sturnidae).

ORIGIN — India, Burma, Ceylon, southeast Asia, Malay Peninsula, Indonesia and the Philippines.

COLOUR
- **Mature:**
  - mostly glossy black with yellow lappets or wattles (featherless skin areas on the sides and back of the head).
  - beak and feet are also yellow, and there is a white patch on each wing.
- **Immature:**
  - smaller wattles; plumage not glossy.

SEXING
- **Mature:**
  - both sexes look alike.
  - males are slightly larger and have a bolder stance; also have longer skin flaps on the neck than females.

WEIGHT — 160–180 gm.

SIZE — 30–45 cm (12–18 in.) in length.

LIFE SPAN — up to 25 years.

DIET — see p. 140.

BREEDING — attempts at breeding mynahs in captivity have not been too successful; they require large quantities of live food when rearing young.

SEASON — spring and summer.

BROOD SIZE — 3 blue-green, brown-spotted eggs, will hatch in 14 days.
— brood leaves the nest at 4 weeks.

NEST TYPE — will accept a cockatiel nest box with twigs, straw or leaves as nesting material.

CAGE TYPE — galvanized metal or stainless steel is best; should also have a false wire bottom.
— rectangular; minimum size of 18 cubic feet, 2′× 3′× 3′.

There are 2 species and 10 subspecies of Indian Hill Mynahs, the Greater and the Lesser. The Greater is the best talker. Most aviculturists agree that the mynah is the finest talking bird available to bird lovers. They make wonderful pets.

If properly cared for, mynahs will live for as long as 25 years – long enough to see your children grow up and have children of their own. Mynahs are best obtained at an age younger than six months. This is the easiest time to tame them and encourage them to talk, and you will find that both sexes learn equally well. Often these birds will not only talk, but also go on to mimic other sounds they frequently hear around them such as a dog's bark, the flush of a toilet or a ringing doorbell.

Mynahs require a large volume of food, although they are not seed-eaters. Given their short digestive tracts and their lusty appetite for food and water, mynahs tend to be messy birds. They pass an abundance of droppings, which is rather hard on their cages. This is why a durable metal should be sought. There are also a number of advantages to a false wire bottom in the cage. For one, it keeps the bird out of its own mess, and then it acts as a platform for things like the open paper bag or privacy box that the mynah enjoys sleeping in.

Daily bathing is important to mynahs. They love to bathe, preferably in 3.5–5 cm (1½–2 in.) of water; and a bath in the morning will allow the bird to dry off during the day when it is most active.

Although the causes are not fully understood, some mynahs have experienced convulsions that are similar to epileptic seizures. Sunlight and vitamin-mineral deficiencies in the diet may be contributing factors to this condition. A well-balanced diet will help to prevent this problem.

TOUCANS AND TOUCANETTES (Plate 14)

FAMILY — Ramphastidae.
ORIGIN — southern Mexico, Central and South America.
COLOUR **Mature:** – variety of colour combinations comprising blue, black, white, yellow, red, green, orange and brown.
– all have large colourful beaks.
Immature: – same; colours are slightly duller.
SEXING — both sexes look alike.
WEIGHT — 175–1000 gm.
SIZE — Toucans: 40–45 cm (16–18 in.) in length.
— Toucanettes: 37.5–42.5 cm (15–17 in.) in length.

	— Aracaris: 35–40 cm (14–16 in.) in length.
LIFE SPAN	— 15–25 years.
DIET	— see p. 140.
BREEDING	— will occasionally breed in captivity.
BROOD SIZE	— 2 white eggs will hatch in 20–25 days.
	— brood leaves the nest at 6–8 weeks.
SEASON	— spring and summer.
NEST TYPE	— large nest boxes or palm logs should be provided.
CAGE TYPE	— do best in large aviaries; should be kept in as large a cage as possible.
	— rectangular; minimum size of 18 cubic feet, 2′× 3′× 3′.

This family group includes some 5 genera, and 40 species. The birds are very colourful, both in looks and personality. Their outstanding feature is a large, lightweight beak that is hollow inside. They make charming, affectionate pets. The delicate manner in which they handle their large beaks is both funny and fascinating. From watching their antics, one would guess they were natural born comics.

These birds do not talk or sing, and are seldom vocal except when they feel hungry or want attention. Their harsh call has a somewhat grating, monotonous quality, but their quiet chuckle is so infectious, it is always a pleasure to overhear.

Toucanettes are smaller than toucans: their bodies and beaks are more slender. The aracaris are related to both, but distinguished by the pronounced serrations to the bill. It takes more time and patience to tame the toucans and toucanettes than it does parrots. But the extra time you invest in them is amply rewarded by the rich character of these birds. The wild streak in the aracaris is also difficult to tame, and in fact success has only come with hand-raised birds. The captured adults remain wild.

These big, healthy birds are inclined to be messy, so that daily cage cleaning is recommended. In an aviary situation, they enjoy the company of other large, soft-billed birds, but should be watched for their tendency to "boss about" the others and perhaps prevent them from eating. If given the opportunity they consume small birds and eggs.

DOMESTIC PIGEONS (Plate 15)

SPECIES	— *Columba livia* (Family Columbidae).	
ORIGIN	— originated in Eurasia; now found all over the world.	
COLOUR	**Mature:**	– basic colour is dull grey with white rump and two large black wing bars; other colours include white, brown, grey, bronzy-green and black.

	Immature:	– basic colour same as adult, but duller.
SEXING	**Mature:**	– males are usually larger, puff their chest out more, strut, and are more vocal.
	Immature:	– difficult to differentiate.

WEIGHT — 300–450 gm.

SIZE — 25–37 cm (10–15 in.) in length.

LIFE SPAN — 10–14 years.

DIET — see p. 141.

MOULTING — usually experience first moult before 6 months of age; mature birds have annual fall moults.

BREEDING — are easy to breed in captivity, but require privacy and a darkened area to nest in.

— once the male has picked the nest site, he will keep all other birds away; he then attracts a female and keeps her near the nest until she lays her eggs.

— only breeding pairs should be kept in the nesting area, a precaution that will lessen the egg damage that invariably results from cockfights. Remove unpaired birds.

— both sexes help incubate the eggs. The parents may breed again when the babies are about 3 weeks old; the male will take charge of feeding the young babies while the hen sits on her new eggs. The female generally incubates the eggs at night, the male during the day, and both females and males manufacture crop milk for their newly hatched young.

— pigeons are capable of breeding at 6 months, but should not be bred until they are one year of age.

SEASON — any time during the spring or summer months.

BROOD SIZE — 2 white eggs, will hatch in 14–19 days.

— brood leaves the nest at 5 weeks.

NEST TYPE — clay flower pot saucers are sufficient, with hay or straw nesting material.

CAGE TYPE — varies with type of pigeon: racing pigeons are kept in lofts that allow them complete liberty. Utility pigeons are generally kept in pens or cages that have a fenced-in open area; Toys are similarly housed, but the unit is a low design to prevent flying, and protect their elaborate plumage.

The pigeon has been a friend of man since 3000 B.C. Our domestic pigeon descends from the ancient Rock Dove, which may originally have been captured and raised as a food source.

Pigeons are faithful creatures. They mate for life, and are reluctant to accept a new mate if their original partner is lost. This same impulse toward one attachment will ultimately bind a pigeon to its owner, and bring the released pigeon home again. Many become just as possessive about their territorial space as about their mate, and will defend each against sudden danger or incursions by other birds.

The popularity of pigeons is as much due to their endless diversity as to their pleasing personalities. Pigeons come in so many colour combinations, they rival the budgies and canaries for capturing the rainbow, and their plumage variations can give them anything from muffed feet to a crested, maned or hooded look. Pigeons have a quiet nature, some coo and some laugh. As a general rule, they are easily tamed and little trouble to care for.

There are over 400 breeds of pigeons, and these are grouped in four basic categories. Utility pigeons are those raised as meat or eating birds because of their heavy breasts and bigger bodies. Flying pigeons are the brilliant air performers, and they include rollers and tumblers – pigeons that whirl, spin and somersault through the air – and tipplers that are capable of high, sustained flight in flocks. Racing Homers are bred for their swiftness, endurance and homing ability. Toy pigeons are the fancy-shaped and colourful show birds: the fantails, pouters, archangels and so on. This last is the largest category.

The choice of housing for pigeons depends on their type (see chart). But, in general, their owner must make a special effort to keep the birds' food, grit and water dishes clean, and clear of droppings. Otherwise, pigeons tend to create a messy environment. They enjoy bathing a great deal and should be given fresh water daily. The pigeon fancier is also careful to avoid overcrowding in the pens or lofts, in order to control the spread of disease and parasites.

The care, feeding, and housing of doves and wild pigeons are very similar to domestic pigeons, and like their domestic cousins, they also do well in aviaries.

CHINESE PAINTED QUAIL (Plate 16)

SPECIES — *Excalfactoria chinensis* (Family Phasianidae).

ORIGIN — India, south-eastern China, Taiwan, Sri Lanka and Formosa.

COLOUR **Mature:**
- feet and legs are orange; beak is mostly black with grey extending down the middle of both sides. Eyes are a deep burgundy colour. Rest of body is a mottled brown colour.
- have two distinct colour phases: normal, which is the browny phase, and silver, where the browns are replaced by a silvery grey colour.

	Immature:	– same as adults.
SEXING	**Mature:**	– male has a broad, flaring, black triangular bib with a white band below, followed by another black band; upper chest and sides are a mixture of light and dark grey with a blue tinge. Underside is a bright chestnut brown with an elliptical band of light buff-white down the centre of the lower chest to the middle of the abdominal area.
		– the female lacks the throat markings and has a rust-coloured abdomen.
	Immature:	– similar in looks, but smaller than adult females; difficult to sex.

WEIGHT — 40–50 gm.
SIZE — 10 cm (4¼ in.) in length.
LIFE SPAN — 6–10 years.
DIET — see p. 141.
BREEDING — breed best if single pairs are placed in an aviary.
— female requires sheltered, private nest or she will lay eggs at random. Other softbill birds should not be in the same cage because they may eat the eggs and offspring.
— female usually lays far more eggs than she can incubate, and hens are often not too fussy about incubating them.
— eggs are large, compared to size of bird; shells are thick and hard. Extra eggs can be hatched in a chick incubator.
— they mature at about 1 year of age.
SEASON — spring and summer.
BROOD SIZE — about 6 bluish-green, brown spotted eggs hatch in 16–18 days;
— brood leaves the nest as soon as they dry off.
NEST TYPE — built on the ground under some secluded cover in the corner of the aviary.
— twigs, straw or leaves for nesting material.
CAGE TYPE — large aviary is best; minimum size of 75 cubic feet, 5′× 5′× 3′, per pair of birds.

Chinese Painted Quail have a very tiny tail that is composed of elongated tail coverts rather than tail feathers as such. They tame easily, are quite gentle and no trouble at all to care for. Their hardy constitutions adapt well to outdoor aviaries, and their peaceful, affectionate natures allow them to get along easily with other species. They also serve a very practical function in an aviary setting: they clean up the seeds dropped by other birds, and eat any insects they happen to find.

Although an amiable little bird, the Chinese painted quail does have distinct traits. It does not, for instance, care much for being handled. When released, it tends to fly upward, to escape, and this may cause injury to the quail's head if you are not careful.

Under certain circumstances, the Chinese painted quail can also become quite fierce. The males will attack members of their own species, which have been newly introduced into the pen, in order to establish their territorial dominance. But as long as suitable hiding places are available for the new members, they can retreat until a more harmonious relationship has had time to develop.

PART II
Bird Diets

The following chapter is composed of diets developed by veterinarians and researchers in avian nutrition.

The first section, excerpted from "Nutrition", by C. Ivar Tollefson in Diseases of Cage and Aviary Birds[1]*, contains diets and general information on the feeding habits of the major bird groups. For each group listed, I have highlighted the recommended diets and suggested the appropriate proportions. You will note three categories: the basic diet, supplemental seeds and mash supplements. The basic diet can be defined as that regular mixture which the mature bird consumes day to day. Supplemental seeds and mash supplements are either mixed with or given in addition to the basic diet during times of physiological stress. These stress periods are the consequence of growth, breeding, moulting or illness.*

You will find that the diets given for budgies, canaries, finches and some of the larger parrots are quite detailed, while those listed for softbills and nectar eaters are less comprehensive. This greater detail simply reflects the length of time these species have been popular, and hence, clinical researchers have had ample opportunity to investigate their nutritional needs. However, a careful reading of the sections on softbills and nectar eaters will give any owner a clear idea of what these species require.

In general, the most important things to remember about bird diets are:

Variety

Birds, like people, get tired of eating the same foods, day in and day out. Offer your bird a variety of foods, and by patient experimentation, you will gradually discover the foods his palate finds acceptable. A bird can eat most of the things people eat, but you should be careful not to spoil its appetite for the nutritious foods it needs.

Freshness

Change your bird's greens and water daily. The bird's seed mixture must always be fresh, and the best test of freshness is to verify that a planted sample will germinate. Many birds leave seed husks in their bowls, and often have difficulty distinguishing whole seeds from the discarded husks. Skimming away these husks, replacing exhausted seed with fresh and cleaning water bowls daily will help keep your bird in strapping good health.

---

1. C. Ivar Tollefson, "Nutrition," in *Diseases of Cage and Aviary Birds*, ed. Margaret L. Petrak, V.M.D. (Philadelphia: Lea & Febiger, 1969), pp. 143–67.

Vitamins

Birds have high metabolic rates – they burn calories very quickly. Therefore, they need regular vitamin and mineral supplements to maintain good health.

– D.A.

FACTORS INFLUENCING CHOICE OF FOOD

It has been suggested[1] that three factors influence a bird's choice of food:

Habit is possibly the strongest factor affecting food selection. The earliest influence comes from the food fed to the chick by its parent. The variety of foods available during the impressionable period after the chick leaves the nest is also highly important in the development of food selection habits.

Appearance is the second factor influencing food selection. A bird has keen eyesight but rather poorly developed senses of taste and smell. Thus it will eat what looks like the food to which it is accustomed. New foods may be regarded with suspicion as potentially dangerous objects. Colour may play a part in this judgment. Whatever the cause, most birds have ultra-conservative eating habits and do not readily change them.

"Personality" may be the third factor influencing food selection. There are definite differences in the ease with which different birds of the same species accept new foods. These personality differences may result from the combined effects of heredity and experience.

BUDGERIGARS

Budgerigars are primarily seed-eaters, although there have been reports that in the wild they eat some insects.[2]

Canary seed (*Phalaris canariensis*) and millet (*Panicum miliaceum*) are the basic components of most diets for budgerigars. The seeds are dehusked in a characteristic fashion and swallowed whole – the discarded husk is not eaten, even when the birds are hungry. Many birds suffer from malnutrition because the owner does not realize that the seed cup is filled with an accumulation of empty husks rather than with whole seeds. The safest way to assure adequate nutrition is to empty the feed cup and refill it with fresh seeds each day.

In laboratory feeding tests (unpublished) budgerigars consumed approximately normal amounts of decorticated canary seed, millet, rape, sesame, and oats when these were fed in the absence of whole seeds. However, when whole and decorticated seeds were supplied simultaneously, the budgerigars showed a distinct preference for the whole seeds.

In free-choice feeding studies over a period of four months, nonbreeding adult budgerigars consumed about 6 gm. of seed and 3 ml. of water per day.[3]

● ● ●

BUDGIES		*Suggested proportions—D.A.*
Basic Diet:	Canary Seed	**– 35 parts**
	Millet	**– 45 parts**
	Rape Seed	**– 5 parts**
	Sesame Seed	**– 5 parts**
	Oats (oat groats or hulled oats)	**– 10 parts**
Supplemental Seeds:	Teazle	**– 20 parts**
	Anise (Aniseed)	**– 20 parts**
	Niger	**– 20 parts**
	Caraway	**– 20 parts**
	Linseed (Flax)	**– 20 parts**
Mash Supplements:	Dried Egg Yolk	**– 25 parts**
	Dried Bakery Product (such as dried brown bread crumbs)	**– 50 parts**
	Lucerne (Alfalfa) Leaf Meal	**– 9 parts**
	Milk protein	**– 5 parts**
	Iodized Salt	**– 0.5 parts**
	Parsley Flakes	**– 5 parts**
a multi vitamin-mineral mix could replace these ingredients	Wheat Germ	**– 2 parts**
	Yeast	**– 2.5 parts**
	Vitamins A, D_3, B_{12}	**– 1 part**

In addition to seeds, budgerigars will consume small amounts of supplementary foods such as greens, vegetables, and mashes. In a two-year study 50 adult nonbreeding budgerigars were maintained in excellent condition on a diet composed of the basic canary seed-millet mix, a supplementary seeds mixture, and a mash supplement.[4] The mash supplement contained dried egg yolk, dried bakery product, lucerne (alfalfa) leaf meal, milk protein, iodized salt, parsley flakes, wheat germ, yeast, vitamins A, D_3 and B_{12}, plus a little canary seed and millet to give the product an appearance more familiar to the birds. The amount of mash supplement consumed was approximately 14 per cent of the total food consumption.

• • •

Although nonbreeding adults can apparently remain in satisfactory condition for long periods on a canary seed-millet mixture, for optimum health it is recommended that supplementary foods be supplied at all times. "Treat" and "Condition Food' products (similar to the supplementary seeds mix and the mash supplement described above), which supply the required protein, vitamin, and mineral supplements, are available in supermarkets and other stores.

● ● ●

If the owner does not wish to use commercial supplemental foods, a number of useful dietary items are available. Greens such as chickweed, dandelion, spinach, carrot tops, and the like are valuable sources of vitamins and minerals. Greens should be washed to remove residues of herbicides and pesticides, and care should be exercised regarding the amount fed, since excessive amounts will cause diarrhoea. Vegetables and fruits such as carrots, celery, and apple may be relished by the birds.

● ● ●

The composition of the different brands of "Treat" and "Condition Food" products may differ considerably – some are merely mixtures of seeds, whereas others may contain supplements of high quality protein, vitamins, and minerals. For example, one brand of "Parakeet Condition Food" lists the following ingredients: millet, oats, canary seed, flax (linseed), soy grits, teazle, and anise seed. The list of ingredients of another brand included: oats, millet, niger, canary seed, caraway, flax (linseed), and sesame seeds, dried bakery product, dried egg yolk, vegetable oil, oyster shell, iodized salt, wheat germ meal, dried whey, alfalfa leaf meal, parsley flakes, Torula dried yeast, vitamin A palmitate, D-activated animal sterol, and vitamin B_{12}. Obviously, these two products are quite different in nutritive value, even though both are labelled "Budgerigar Condition Food." A careful study of the label should indicate the preparation that would supply the most vitamin, mineral, and protein supplements to a normal seed diet.

● ● ●

CANARIES

Canary seed (*Phalaris canariensis*), rape seed (*Brassica rapa*), and millet seed (*Panicum miliaceum*) are the basic components of most canary diets. Many other seeds are also used by fanciers to bring the birds into breeding condition, to tighten and gloss the plumage for exhibition, or to improve colour. Like other seed-eaters, canaries remove the husk and swallow the kernel whole. Grit, cuttlefish bone, and water should be supplied at all times.

• • •

In addition to seed, canaries will consume small quantities of supplementary foods such as greens, vegetables, and mashes. In the study with young canaries,[5] the birds were found to consume an average of 0.34 gm. of a mash supplement per day, this amounting to approximately 10 per cent of the total food consumption. The mash supplement contained bakery crumbs, dried egg yolk, dried milk protein product, wheat germ meal,

CANARIES		*Suggested Proportions—D.A.*
Basic Diet:	Canary Seed	**– 50 parts**
	Rape Seed	**– 30 parts**
	Millet (equal portions of red, white & yellow millet)	**– 20 parts**
Supplemental Seeds:	Teazle	**– 20 parts**
	Anise (Aniseed)	**– 20 parts**
	Niger	**– 20 parts**
	Caraway	**– 20 parts**
	Linseed (Flax)	**– 20 parts**
Mash Supplements:	Bakery Crumbs	**– 50 parts**
	Dried Egg Yolk	**– 20 parts**
	Dried Milk Protein	**– 5 parts**
	Wheat Germ Meal	**– 2 parts**
	Alfalfa Leaf Meal	**– 7 parts**
	Dried Yeast	**– 2.5 parts**
	Parsley Flakes	**– 2 parts**
	Soy Grits	**– 8 parts**
	Vegetable Oil	**– 2 parts**
	Iodized Salt	**– 0.5 parts**
(best supplied as multi vitamin-mineral mix)	Vitamins A, D_3, B_{12}	**– 1 part**

alfalfa leaf meal, dried yeast, parsley flakes, soy grits, vegetable oil, iodized salt, and supplements of vitamins A, D_3, and B_{12}.

• • •

Many nonbreeding adult canaries receive nothing but a seeds mixture and appear to remain in satisfactory condition. However, for optimum health, it is recommended that supplementary foods be supplied at all times. There are various commercially available "Condition Food," "Song Food," and "Moulting Food" products which will supply the required protein, vitamin, and mineral supplements. As with budgerigars, Siegmund[6] suggests that new owners of finch-type birds be advised to feed the packaged products of reliable birdseed firms.

FINCHES

Like canaries, other members of the finch families are mainly seed-eaters, although some species also eat live food on a daily basis, and many others require it at breeding time. The basic diet should therefore consist of a seed mix, dietary supplements, cuttlefish bone, grit, and water .

The seed mix for finches generally contains millets, canary seed, and occasionally oats. The larger finches do well on a budgerigar seed mix.[7]

• • •

The dietary supplements may include commercial "Budgerigar" or "Canary Condition Food," green food, fruits, and live food. "Mynah Food" or softbill meal (see section on "Feeding of Softbills, or Insect-Eaters") may be used to supply the insect requirements of many finches. Outdoor flight spaces are often planted with shrubs to attract insects as well as to beautify the space.

• • •

Small insects are very useful dietary items, especially during breeding. Small mealworms, gentles (maggots of the blowfly or bluebottle fly), spiders, and small flies are generally accepted readily. A fine-grade softbill meal is also very valuable.

• • •

There is still much to be learned about the exact food requirements of finches. It would seem that a varied diet, with provision of an ample supply

FINCHES		*Suggested Proportions—D.A.*
Basic Diet:	Canary Seed	**– 35 parts**
	Millet (equal portions of red, white & yellow millet)	**– 45 parts**
	Oats (oat groats or hulled oats)	**– 6 parts**
	Rape Seed	**– 7 parts**
	Sesame Seed	**– 7 parts**
Supplemental Seeds:	Teazle	**– 20 parts**
	Anise (Aniseed)	**– 20 parts**
	Niger	**– 20 parts**
	Caraway	**– 20 parts**
	Linseed (Flax)	**– 20 parts**
Other Supplements:	Small Mealworms Cleaned Maggots Spiders Small Flies	2–6 per day; the higher number to be fed during breeding season

of high quality protein, vitamins and minerals, would be the best means of ensuring health and longevity of the birds.

SOFTBILL OR INSECT EATERS

Different species of soft-billed birds vary in their food requirements. Swallows (Hirundinidae) eat practically nothing but insects; tanagers (Thraupidae) eat mainly fruit and some insects; thrushes (Turdidae) eat small fruits, insects and seeds; pigeons and doves (Columbidae) feed almost entirely on seeds.

Aviculturists have repeatedly stressed the desirability of feeding insectivorous birds large quantities of a variety of live foods, such as flies, spiders, worms, moths, snails, butterflies, beetles, and cockroaches. Insectivorous birds obviously are adapted physiologically to the nutritional elements composing insects which render the natural items more valuable than the most elaborate laboratory foods. The insects are swallowed whole by some birds, with any chitinous parts being cast up as pellets. Others remove certain parts, such as the wings.

• • •

SOFTBILL OR INSECT EATERS

In the absence of live insects, commercial insectile mixes are recommended. They usually contain:	Dried Insects Ant Eggs Ground Seeds Suet	feed free choice
	Finely Ground Boiled Beef & Hard Boiled Egg	can be added in small amounts, 2–3 times a week
Mynah bird food is the most common commercial insectile mix.		

If the birds are maintained in an outdoor aviary, insects may be attracted by ripe fruit, meat, or various types of shrubbery. It is desirable to use dwarf shrubs planted in tubs that can be removed from the aviary for cleaning. Softbills do not eat the leaves of shrubbery, and many types of shrubs are suitable for use in aviaries.

Mealworms (*Tenebrio* spp.) have been widely used by fanciers of soft-billed birds. They can be purchased in some pet shops or they may be raised in a simple culture of bran with a little apple or lettuce added to provide moisture. Mealworms are considered a highly concentrated food, and it is recommended that only limited quantities be fed. Too many worms will make the bird fat, and its appetite for other foods will be diminished. A thrush-sized bird might be given 3 to 6 worms per day during the off season, with the amount being doubled or tripled when the bird is in full song. For small soft-billed birds, small mealworms should be used, or large meal-worms should be placed in boiling water for a few minutes to soften the skin and then they should be cut into small pieces.[8]

Bee larvae (*Apis mellifera*) are considered excellent food for softbills. They were readily accepted by American goldfinch fledglings (*Spinus tristis*), and were used as a base for hand-rearing of Traills' flycatchers (*Empidonax traillii*). Methods of culturing bee larvae were described by Gary *et al.*[9]

Although it may be possible to purchase, capture, or culture some live food, it will generally be necessary to use an "insectile food" as partial replacement for live food. Various commercial preparations known as mynah food, softbill meal, or insectile food are available. Such products may contain dried insects, ant eggs, ground seeds, suet, and other materials suitable for softbills. The mix is usually moistened with freshly grated carrot or apple to make a crumbly, but not wet, mass before it is fed to the birds. Some finely ground boiled beef or hard-boiled egg may be added. Various fresh fruits in season are usually given separately.[10]

For those who wish to mix their own insectile foods, a number of formulas are available. Ficken and Dilger[11] kept several species of thrush (Turdidae) in perfect condition on an inexpensive mixture consisting of equal parts of dog meal, dried flies, and turkey or chick starter mash. The three components are mixed with cottonseed oil until slightly moist, which greatly increased palatability of the mixture. After it is mixed the food should be used in a few days, because the unsaturated fatty acids of the cottonseed oil cause oxidation of vitamin E and to a lesser extent of vitamin A; this oxidizing tendency may be essentially eliminated by addition of an antioxidant.

The following formula by T.G. Taylor was reported by Carr[12].

3½ lb. fine biscuit meal or sausage rusk
8 oz. dry whole milk
8 oz. wheat germ
8 oz. white fish meal
4 oz. dried yeast
½ oz. Adexolin (vitamins A and D) in 5 oz. peanut oil.

The whole mixture should have a crumbly consistency when fed.

Another formula, reported by Tanner,[13] consists of the combination of two mixtures:

A. Combine 4 oz. ant eggs
4 oz. dried flies or shrimp meal
3 oz. melted drippings
B. Combine 8 oz. powdered rich tea biscuits
3 oz. melted honey
3 oz. egg powder.

Mix A and B. A little cod liver oil and Bemax cereal may be added. A useful but perishable addition to this mixture is finely scraped raw meat made into small pellets.

In the wild, insectivorous birds search continually for food; they must capture it or starve. They seem to be psychologically adapted to eating whenever food is available. When such birds are given food *ad libitum*, they tend to overeat and quickly become obese. This problem is much more serious in birds kept in cages than in those kept in aviaries. According to Dilger, the only solution seems to be restriction of the amount of food made available to the bird. Woodward[14] also observed that aviary life is too easy, and that soft-billed birds in captivity have a great tendency to overeat and become obese.

In addition to live food and 'insectile mix," there are many food items which may be used to give variety in the menu. Hard-boiled eggs may be mashed and mixed with the insectile food or fed separately. Peanut butter is relished by many softbills. Precooked baby cereal or sponge cake can be mixed with milk to form a nutritious thick mush. Fruits of various kinds form an essential element in the daily diet of nearly every softbill.[15] Some authors recommend using only sweet, ripe fruits, and caution against the use of tart or unripe fruits.

FRUIT & NECTAR EATERS

This group of birds includes lories and lorikeets (Psittacidae), toucans, toucanettes, and aracaris (Ramphastidae), hummingbirds (Trochilidae), sunbirds (Nectariniidae), honey-eaters (Meliphagidae), white-eyes (Zosteropidae), honeycreepers (Coerebidae), and flower-peckers (Dicaeidae). These birds feed on the sugary liquids (nectar) found in the corolla of flowers and on the insects found in or with the nectar. In addition, sweet ripe fruit is an important part of their diet.

FRUIT & NECTAR EATERS

Basic Diet:	Mellin's Food	1 Tsp.	
	Evaporated Milk	1 Tsp.	in 1 cup
	Honey	1 Tsp.	of water
	Sweet Fruit		free choice

Lories and lorikeets of the subfamily Loriinae of the family Psittacidae and other nectar-feeding species may be fed nectar composed of Mellin's Food,* evaporated milk, and honey (1 teaspoonful of each in 1 cup of water), plus sweet fruit. In addition, some species will eat canary seed and sunflower seed.[16] For lories and lorikeets Bronson[17] suggests brown or wild rice boiled in milk, with brown sugar or honey added. Fruits may be mixed with mashed potato. Fruit cake, sponge cake, or whole wheat bread soaked in milk and sweetened with honey is valuable. Fresh fruits, berries, canned baby food, and canned fruit salad are also recommended. The food dishes should be washed daily and refilled with fresh material.

There are a number of formulas for nectar, many of them being based on Mellin's Food, condensed milk, and honey. The New York Zoological Park uses two different formulas for feeding hummingbirds:

Formula A:

Mellin's Food	4 teaspoons
Honey	5 teaspoons
Condensed milk	1 teaspoon
Beef extract	5 ml.
Vitamins (Multiple)	4 drops
Warm water	1 quart

Formula B:

Honey	5 teaspoons
Beef extract	5 ml.
Vitamins (Multiple)	4 drops
Warm water	1 quart

A ruby-throated hummingbird (*Archilocus colubris*) weighing 2.5 gm. consumed 121.8 ml. of formula in 7 days: 112 ml. of formula A fed in the morning and 9.8 ml. of formula B fed in the evening.[18]

Sunbirds were fed the following diet at the London Zoo[19]: nectar food, grapes, and a few mealworms. The nectar food was made by mixing 1 level dessertspoonful of baby food, 1 heaped dessertspoonful of sweetened condensed milk, and 1½ dessertspoonfuls of honey with ¾ pint of boiling water. (A dessertspoonful equals 8 ml.)

Honey milk sop (sponge cake or precooked cereal moistened with milk and sweetened with honey) is a valuable dietary item for some members of this group. Fresh fruit, berries, canned baby food, or canned fruit salad may also be used.

If the fruit – and nectar-eaters can be kept in a large, well-planted aviary, some nectar may be available from the flowers, which will also attract insects. Ripe fruit is often used to attract insects, such as fruit flies (*Drosophila* spp.)

References

1. Lafeber, T.J.: Nutrition of the Budgerigar (Melospittacus undulatus) Animal Hospital I: 276–287, 1965.
2. Worden, A.N.: Focus on budgerigar nutrition. Cage Birds 116: 145–147, 1959.
3. Bice, C.W.: Observations on budgie feeding. Budgerigar Bulletin No. 113, pp. 19–27, 1956.
4. Bice, C.W. ibid.
5. Bice, C.W.: Millets for cage birds. All-Pets Magazine 26 (3): 72–84 and 26 (4): 109–126, 1955.
6. Siegmund, O.H., ed: The Merck Veterinary Manual, 2nd ed. Rahway, N.J., Merck & Co., Inc., 1961. Management of Caged Birds, pp. 1394–1399.
7. Dilger, C.W.: Personal communications, 1963.
8. Naether, C.: Soft-Billed Birds. Fond du Lac, Wis., All-Pets Books Inc., 1955.
9. Gary, N.E., Ficken, R.W., and Stein R.C.: Honey Bee Larvae (Apis mellifera L.) for bird food. Avic, Mag. 67: 27–32, 1961.

---

*Mellin's Food: a maltose dextrin mixture with added thiamine mononitrate, ferric glycerol phosphate, and potassium bicarbonate.

10. Naether, C. see 8 above.
11. Ficken, R.W., and Dilger, W.C.: Insects and food mixtures for insectivorous birds. Avic. Mag. 67: 46–55, 1961.
12. Carr, V.A. V.: Topical comment. Cage & Aviary Birds 127: 512, 1965.
13. Tanner, E.B.: Breeding Foreign Softbills. Cage & Aviary Birds 125: 313, 1964.
14. Woodward, I.D.: Catering for Softbills. Cage & Aviary Birds 128: 6, 1965.
15. Naether, C. see 8 above.
16. Plath, K., and Davis, M.: Parrots Exclusively. Fond du Lac, Wis., All-Pets Books Inc., 1957. p. 9.
17. Bronson, J.L.: Parrot Family Birds, rev. 3rd ed. Fond du Lac, Wis., All-Pets Books Inc., 1957. p. 36.
18. Spector, W.C., ed.: Handbook of Biological Data. Philadelphia, W.B. Saunders Co., 1956 p. 213.
19. Tanner, E.B.: Old World gems. Cage & Aviary Birds 129: 225–226, 1966.

COCKATIELS, PARROTS & MACAWS

This diet (see p. 138) was formulated by Dr. Greg J. Harrison, president of the Research Center for Avian Medicine, Nutrition and Reproduction in Lake Worth, Florida. Dr. Harrison developed this "maintenance diet" to offer birds a nutritious, varied diet that is simple for owners to prepare and store.

– D.A.

Harrison comments on his maintenance diet:

Introducing the Diet

– if the bird is resisting these new foods, remove the sunflower seeds in the morning, but leave the monkey biscuit, sprouts, seedlings and cheese. In late afternoon, return the bird's sunflower seeds. After a few days of this routine, the bird should grow accustomed to the new foods and accept them. Gradually the bird will consume less and less dry seed as it begins to prefer the sprouts.

Weight Gain

– in this case, reduce the bird's intake of high-energy foods, for instance the sunflower seeds, cheese and sprouts.

Vitamin Supplements

– on this diet, vitamins are only supplied during times of "high stress" or illness. We recommend: the 6.4 oz. package of Head-start poultry vitamins mixed with 30 methacholine capsules, or commercially available mixtures like Avia, and 8 in 1. Check the label to make sure it contains methionine, choline, the inositol. Sprinkle the vitamin powder over the bird's favourite food. During moults, you can also increase the bird's intake of cheese and monkey biscuit (for the extra protein it needs during this stressful period).

BABY COCKATIELS, PARROTS, MACAWS & COCKATOOS

Basic Diet (suggested by Dr. Harrison)

Science Diet® monkey biscuit, available in pet supply stores, is a quality food source for all psittacine birds.[1] It is also a valuable component in the diets of baby psittacines. The following baby mix is recommended:

Monkey Biscuits	– 35
Cups Water	– 3
Cup Carnation Powdered Milk	– 1/3
Sunflower or Corn Oil	– 2tsp.

Mix in a blender and bake in a microwave oven until it just pours.

PARROTS, MACAWS & COCKATOOS

The following diet was developed by Dr. Raymond A. Kray, an avian specialist from Burbank, California. Dr. Kray, who is actively involved in avian nutrition research, has found that this mixture appeals to most members of the parrot family.

– D.A.

Basic Soft Food Diet:

Dry Dog Kibble (20% protein) pulverized or blended	1 part
Boiled Rice	1 part
Canned or Boiled Beans (Kidney, Lima or Pinto)	1 part
Canned or Fresh Corn	1 part

To increase palatability, boil rice and beans in water containing chicken or beef bouillon cubes. After mixing all 4 ingredients, add a little honey, oregano or garlic flakes. Freeze in small daily portions in plastic bags. Feed by mixing ¼ cup of mixture with ¼ cup of sunflower seed, 1/8th teaspoon of dicalcium phosphate, and ¼ teaspoon of dry multiple vitamin and amino acid mixture. This combination should supply about 75% of the total

1. Science Diet®, or ZuPreem® Primate Dry monkey biscuit is made by Hills, a division of Riviana Foods.

volume eaten by the bird. The other 25% should consist of fruits, vegetables, cheese and cooked meat scraps.[2]

As it is very difficult to get birds to eat a balanced diet by feeding seeds, due to their selective feeding activity, this soft food diet provides a much better balance of nutrients. Feed this diet fresh each day. – *D.A.*

ADULT/CAGED BIRD MAINTENANCE DIET

FOOD		FREQUENCY	AMOUNTS PER BIRD		
			Cockatiel	Amazon	Macaw
MONKEY BISCUIT	(ZuPreem® Primate Dry): Soaked for 30 seconds or dry.	Fresh Daily	1	2	4
SPROUTS[1]	*Mixture:* 25% sunflower seeds; 45% Canadian peas; 15% Parrakeet (Budgie) mix; Canary seed. *Soak:*[2] Drain and rinse 3 times; spread to dry on draining bed. Rinse 3 times during second 24 hours.[3] Feed when root tip shows. Can store three days in sprouter or week in refrigerator; rinse prior to feeding.	Fresh Daily	1 Tbsp.	2 Tbsp.	4 Tbsp.
SEEDLINGS	3″ Sunflower plants (or dark greens like spinach).	Fresh Daily	2	4	8
FRESH CORN ON THE COB		Fresh Daily	¼″ piece	½″ piece	1″ piece
FRUIT	Apple Orange	Fresh Daily Twice Weekly	will not eat will not eat	1/12 1/12	1/6 1/6
CHEESE		Fresh Daily	size of a pea	½ Tbsp.	1 Tbsp.
DRY SEEDS	1 feeding cup of sunflower seeds 1 feeding cup of small seed mixture (60% Canary/40% Parrakeet [Budgie]).	Daily Daily	1 Tbsp. ”	2 Tbsp. ”	4 Tbsp. ”
MINERAL SUPPLEMENTS	Cuttlebone and/or 8 in 1 Parrakeet Mineral Treat Block® (aviary size). Salt mineral block (produced for Rabbits).	Always Available			

[1] Any seeds that show less than 80% sprouting should not be fed. [2] The soaking/sprouting time period will depend on environmental temperatures. [3] Sprinkle sprouting seeds with calcium carbonate or crushed mineral bone. Three times yearly, add a grit mineral mix (use ½ cup of the grit mineral mixture per gallon of sprouts, or 1½ teaspoons per cup). For small amounts use a paper cup and poke holes in bottom for drainage.

COCKATOOS, PARROTS, MACAWS & CONURES (a)
(suggested by Dr. Axelson)

Basic Diet:

Safflower seed	10 parts
Sunflower seed	25 parts
Shelled Walnuts	2 parts
Shelled Brazil Nuts	2 parts
Raw Peanuts	3 parts
Niger seed	1 part
Rape seed	2 parts
Dry Dog Kibble or Zu Preem® monkey biscuit[3]	15 parts
White Millet	5 parts
Cracked Corn	10 parts
Oat Groats	10 parts
Canary seed	10 parts
Turkey pellets	5 parts

This basic seed mix can be fed free choice along with daily portions of fruit, vegetables and greens.

Liquid vitamin – mineral mix in drinking water	– daily

– *D.A.*

COCKATIELS, PARRAKEETS, & LOVE BIRDS
(suggested by Dr. Axelson)

These birds will thrive on the foods listed below. I have included suggestions on feeding frequency and suitable methods of presenting these foods to your bird.

– *D.A.*

Basic Diet:

Budgie basic seed mix (p. 127)	– 85 parts
Milo	– 5 parts
Sunflower Seed	– 5 parts
Safflower Seed	– 5 parts

Larger birds need seed variety (use (a) mix above)	– separate seed dish
Budgie treat food (& supplement seeds)	– twice weekly (daily when stressed)

2. Originally published in *Bird World*, October–November 1978.
3. Manufacted by Hill's – Division of Riviana Foods, Topeka, Kansas.

Fruit, Vegetables & Greens	– daily
Liquid Vitamin-Mineral (in drinking water)	– daily
Grit & ground White Oyster Shell	– free choice

MYNAHS

(Suggested by Dr. Axelson)

Basic Diet:

Chopped mixed fruit (any kind)	– 35 parts
Commercial mynah pellets or mash	– 40 parts
Fine consistency canned dog food	– 25 parts
Insects such as mealworms, crickets or fly larvae	– 2–3 times a week
Diced hard boiled egg	– ½ egg weekly
Vitamin-mineral powder in mash or fruit mix	– daily

TOUCANS AND TOUCANETTES

(Suggested by Dr. Axelson)

Basic Diet:

Chopped mixed fruits (any kind)	– 45 parts
Commercial mynah pellets	– 25 parts
Canned dog food chopped fine	– 30 parts
Insects such as crickets or mealworms	– twice weekly
Baby mice or chopped adult mice	– weekly
Whole wheat bread soaked in skim milk and diced hard boiled egg	– once or twice weekly
Vitamin-mineral powder added to fruit or dog food	– daily
Can also feed parrot soft food diet (chopped fine or it goes through undigested)	– daily

PIGEONS & DOVES

(suggested by M.F. Roberts[4] and Dr. Axelson)

Basic Diet:

Whole Peas	– 10 parts
Whole Corn (small hard corn)	– 20 parts
Kafir	– 10 parts
Red Spring Wheat (well seasoned)	– 10 parts
Rye, Barley, Oat Groats, Peanuts, Buckwheat, Vetch, Linseed (Flax)	feed as a treat food once or twice weekly, up to 10 parts
Commercial Pigeon Pellets	– 50 parts
Grit (plus oyster shell & a little salt)	– free choice
Greens (Watercress, Lettuce, Dandelions)	– daily

CHINESE PAINTED QUAIL

Basic Diet:

Budgie, Canary, or Finch mix	– free choice
Mealworms, or other live food	– 4–6 worms, daily per bird
Grit & ground White Oyster Shell	– free choice
Sprouted seeds	– free choice when nesting.
Liquid Vitamin-Mineral supplement (in drinking water)	– daily

4. *How To Raise and Train Pigeons*, by Mervin F. Roberts. (Neptune City, J.J.: T.F.H. Publications Inc.), pp. 13–15.

AVERAGE WEIGHT FOR PET BIRDS

A healthy adult bird generally maintains a constant weight. Excessive weight may indicate obesity, while a loss in weight may indicate an unwell bird. A decrease in appetite is one of the first signs of ill health, and this will result in some weight loss. In general, a 3% drop in a bird's average weight means that the bird is becoming sick, and some form of proper therapy should be started.[5]

Birds should be weighed with an accurate balance scale, preferably calibrated in grams.[6] *Some veterinarians who treat birds may have these scales, as may some pet shops. Spring scales are not accurate enough to be reliable. The following table will give you some idea of average weights relative to species and bird size.*

SPECIES	WEIGHT	
Budgies	30–35	gms.
Canaries	20	gms.
Finches	10–35	gms.
Small Finches	12	gms.
Medium Parrots	300	gms.
Larger Parrots	450–500	gms.
Love Birds	45–60	gms.
Conures	70–150	gms.
Parrakeets	60–200	gms.
Macaws – small	300–600	gms.
Macaws – large	600–1200	gms.
Parrotlets	35–65	gms.
Cockatoos	300–800	gms.
Cockatiels	80–90	gms.
Lories and Lorikeets	35–200	gms.
Mynah Birds	160–180	gms.
Toucans & Toucanettes	125–1000	gms.
Pigeons	300–450	gms.
Doves	85–350	gms.
Button Quail	40–50	gms.

PELLETED FOODS

Over the last two or three years there have been several pelleted diets developed, which according to the manufacturers are "complete diets". The concept of a pelleted food is not new as it has been used for years in

5. T.J. Lafeber, D.V.M. "On Pet Birds" in Pet Age Magazine, monthly, Chicago, Vol. 8, 5 (Nov., 1979), p. 30.
6. These scales are available from Dorothy Products, 7278 Milwaukee Avenue, Niles, Illinois 60648.

feeding poulty, and various animals. Since captive birds do not have the desire or perhaps the intelligence to eat the variety of foods they should, even if they are presented, then a complete diet in the form of a pellet does make a lot of sense.

There are pellets available for a variety of avian species and there are maintenance diets, growth diets and breeding diets. The nutritional requirements will vary at different times and the appropriate type should be fed as it is needed. Fruits, vegetables and greens can also be fed along with the pellets.

It may take a bit of persistence, but most birds can be trained to eat the pellets. Breeders that are using this food form are finding that the birds are generally thriving on it.

Pellets impregnated with 1% tetracycline are available and are being used in some of the quarantine stations in the USA.

The droppings from birds on pelleted foods may be a browny colour with white urates which is normal and should not be confused with abnormal dropping colour.

Controlling Bird Behaviour

Most pet owners will agree that a trained pet is a pleasure to have around. The object of training is not to alter a pet's personality, but rather to communicate a certain standard of behaviour within which the bird can be his own character.

The collected articles in this section describe various techniques that have been developed to tame and train pet birds. "The Squawking Bird" outlines a rather humorous method for quieting "squawkers", but reminds the reader that shrieking is instinctual in many large birds – something you may have to live with.

The article on "Gang Taming" elaborates a very humane method of taming wild birds. In principle, these trainers object to the use of restraints or any method that forces a bird's will, and instead, try to create a situation that encourages the bird to approach humans voluntarily. In a similar vein, "Taming Parrots: Questions and Answers" describes the simple gestures of friendship, the patience, and the lack of hurry that altogether woo a bird to tameness.

It is hoped that in reading these articles you may find new insights into the ways and means of gently curbing and controlling your pet's behaviour.

– D.A.

"THE SQUAWKING BIRD"

. . . the least attractive part of an active bird is [its] tendency to scream and bray. Birds like to scream, especially amazons, macaws, cockatoos and some conures. If you understand this going in and are prepared to live with it, you won't be so unhappy when you discover this facet of their personalities.

Most birds, even hard cases, can be modified in their habits of noise, but it is a natural part of the avian beast to make noise. He is a creature of the forests and jungles, and screams are a part of that life.

Before I go into training a bird not to scream, let me say that I do so only to prevent people from dumping their birds because the noise has become intolerable. My first . . . [instinct is to say] that if you can't take the noise, don't get a parrot . . .

If all else is perfect, and your only problem is a bird that has screaming fits, or has a habit of screaming all day while you are out and is bringing threats from the neighbours, there is help.

Read the method over several times before starting the training and rehearse it so that you do not make any mistakes.

"The Squawking Bird," *Bird World*, August-September 1979, p. 21. Reprinted with the permission of the publisher.

This training will not work, and should not be used if you have several birds. The only way to use this method is to train one bird at a time with no other birds present.

• • •

The method is chain-training. The theory is that the bird is reprimanded by an object not seemingly associated with you, and one that he cannot punish by a bite.

You will need several small lengths of lightweight brass chain, the kind used for swag lamps. It must be brass. Part of the training involves the distinctive sound of brass chain as it jingles, so substitutes are useless.

The chain pieces (three links each) should be suspended over the birds' cage by high-test fishline or clear leader. The other end of the line is then strung to a remote location where you or someone else can release it.

Most birds are trained with only one or two tries, so don't expect to make this a lifelong project.

You must arrange the training so that the bird does not suspect that you have control over the chain. Birds are very smart, and if he suspects a trick you have lost.

He must think that the chain has a mind of its own, and that the only time anything happens is when he screams. It is at that point that he will decide himself that he doesn't want to scream.

Never allow the chain to hit the bird. It is sufficient that it only drop close to him. The small pieces are used in the event that if one accidentally hits the bird, there will be no pain.

Affix two or three chains above the cage, situated so that when the line is released the chains will drop on the edge of the cage and make a noise. You should also be able to raise the chain and re-set it, from your remote station.

If the bird screams with you present, have someone in the next room release a chain as soon as the screaming begins. If there is no reaction, release the second chain. By then the bird will have discovered that something has happened and will stop screaming, if only for a second or two.

Leave the chains where they fall, and wait a bit. If the bird starts again to scream, lift the chains so that they once again make noise. This time on their way up. If he remains quiet, go to his cage and gently remove the chains and, in [co-operation] with the person in the next room, re-set them over the cage.

The most frequent reaction is silence. If the silence lasts for a couple of minutes, give the bird some food treat that will occupy his mouth with something other than vocalizing.

• • •

You might have to [stand by patiently] . . . that first day and wait for him to test the waters again. After some time, curiosity will get the better of him and he will start again. If the same thing happens, he will be convinced that it is directly related to his voice, and you have a trained bird.

● ● ●

The chain should not be left in his cage to chew on or play with, the fishline, especially if it is plastic, must be removed immediately as it is dangerous for him to chew on.

Once training has begun, he will know that there is a distinctive sound that accompanies the chain. It is the jingle of brass. Once he associates this sound with a reprimand, it is possible to have pieces of chain in your pocket or in the table, and the mere movement of the chain and the sound of the jingle will be enough to cause him to quiet down. . . .

If you only care if the bird is quiet while you are home, and you have no problem with neighbours, it is permissible for him to know that you control the chain. He will then learn that even though you are the one that activates the chain, you only do it when he screams. . . .

This training must be reinforced with a positive reward. If he is quiet and good, offer him some special treat.

One last comment. Many times screaming is caused by an unhappy bird. Many times, if the water is kept fresh and clean, and the food is varied and interesting, and the cage is cleaned daily, a former screamer becomes quiet and happy. The first thing to check if your bird screams, is food and water. The problem may be only your own neglect.

"GANG TAMING"

This commercial taming method was developed by Henry Rosen and Joe Venturini of Tame Birds Inc., North Hollywood, California. Both men are experienced bird handlers and trainers. While this method was designed for taming a large number of birds in a short period of time, its techniques are effective for individual birds as well.

— *D.A.*

[After] the [imported] birds are released from quarantine [a mandatory period of 30 days] they are placed into conditioning. The birds are fed a combination of cracked corn, rolled wheat, barley and oats. This food is cooked and given to the birds with a powdered protein supplement. Occasionally the birds will be kept on tetracycline an additional 15 days, so that the sum total of treatment is a full 45 days.

The birds are purchased in lots [and for taming purposes] . . . are sorted into groups of about 10 birds . . . usually all the same species. As one or two groups are being tamed, others are being conditioned and prepared for later training. The condition[ing] and taming is timed so that as the birds [become tame] . . . they are also in good feather and weight, and ready for resale.

"Gang Taming," *Bird World*, April–May 1979, p. 26. Reprinted with the permission of the publisher.

On the day I visited Tame Birds, Henry Rosen was working with a group of about eight mexican redheads. The birds were kept in wire cages that hung on one wall. Water was in all cages, but no food dishes. During training all birds are kept from free-feeding.

Mr. Rosen explained that birds are truly tame when they will come to you. He rarely forces his training on any bird. The theory is that these birds have been grabbed, netted, caged, shipped, and that the last thing they need is to have someone grab them again and force obedience.

After a period of building up the bird, the actual training begins. . . .

[The birds] have been well-fed and are [a] good weight . . . so the time that it takes for the bird to get over his resistance to hand-feeding is not harmful in any way. It is never more than a day. As a last resort, the trainer can use a [trained]bird . . . to show the newcomers what to do. Parrots learn much by watching other birds, and using a trained bird is an easy way to get the rest started.

As I watched, Mr. Rosen opened all of the [bird] cages . . . and placed a long rod [between] the bottom cage [and] . . . a card table. He then sat to one side with sunflower seed in his hand.

He put a bit of the seed on the table and sat playing with a handful, pouring it from one hand to the other, intriguing the birds.

First one, then another, then another began climbing out of the cages and down the tiers onto the table. They came readily to Mr. Rosen. The birds had been in training about three days. The sessions take place about five times a day, so there is plenty of opportunity to eat.

The birds clucked and muttered to each other, and went straight for the food. As the birds ate, Mr. Rosen coaxed one of the birds onto his hand by slowly moving the hand with the food away from the table, and placing his empty hand in front of it. If the bird wished to continue [eating] . . . he had to step onto Mr. Rosen's hand to do so. The bird was not at all hesitant . . . He trusted Mr. Rosen, the bird came to him. To illustrate the effectiveness of this training method, Mr. Rosen put a sunflower seed in his mouth . . . It was the first time he had attempted this with these birds, [and] I could see that he was ready to withdraw in a moment, but the bird was only concerned with the food and took the seed gently.

As Mr. Rosen worked with the first bird, the other birds on the table leaned out toward him to see what was happening. They were curious and ready to do what the other bird was doing in order to share in the food. Before the end of the session, several birds had climbed onto Mr. Rosen's hand, legs and arms in search of food. For the most part, they permitted petting and scratching. The birds who were reluctant to play this game went back up into their own cages, but they soon returned when they saw that the rest of the birds were having a good time and being fed.

I asked Mr. Rosen how long this method takes. He told me that he expected to have each group of birds ready for sale in two weeks from the time he started training.

They train several groups at the same time, in different areas, so have birds working all the time.

This method of taming seems to be quite successful; they offer a 100% guarantee that a dealer buying one of [their] birds can, upon receipt of the bird, expect it to step onto his hand (or his customer's hand), and ride on his shoulder immediately. In a later discussion with Joe Venturini, he explained that one of the problems . . . pet dealers . . . run into . . . is the so-called "tame" birds [that] . . . won't come out of a cage. They have been hauled out for training and may still be fearful of a human approaching . . . and violating their dignity by forcibly removing them from the cage.

With the "Tame Birds' method, the birds are never forced out of their cages. . . . Early in this method of training, the trainers open the cages and offer food to the birds in their own cages. The birds learn that the hand coming at them means no harm. . . . The result is a bird that will step onto a hand with confidence . . .

By the time the birds are ready to be sold, the trainers have handled all of the birds and shown them that they have nothing to fear.

Considering that not all birds have the same temperament, I asked questions regarding those that would not respond, knowing that there must be a few . . .

If a bird totally resists the offer of food, he is put away without food for a couple of hours and is tried later. Mr. Rosen added that if, when offering food, you know that the bird is going for your hand to bite it, try to see that he gets your entire finger in his beak and not just a pinch. If he gets the whole finger, he can only apply pressure – if he gets a chunk in the tip of his beak, it is painful. . . . The trainers will, in extreme cases, grab a bird with a glove. [Mr. Rosen] basically opposes the use of such restraints; he feels the bird has been through enough, and submitting him to the insult of glove or towel restraint can push an otherwise sweet bird over the brink. If you must resort to this method, get rid of it as soon as possible. Use it only to get the bird on your hand, and as soon as he is standing [there], get the glove off and/or the towel away.

● ● ●

I asked about the birds that don't respond [to] getting hungry. Mr. Rosen told me that he has never had a bird that did not eat readily the second day.

"TAMING PARROTS:"

Questions & Answers by Bill Marcus
Mr. Marcus, an experienced bird handler, answers the three questions he is most commonly asked.

– D.A.

After my article on taming appeared in Bird World (February-March 1979), I received many letters and phone calls asking about particular problems [on] taming birds.

The first, most common question is:

"My Parrot still bites me, when will he stop?"
He [the bird] will need time to fully adjust to his surroundings and his life. If you can keep the bird with you as much as possible when you are home it will help. Let the bird climb around on your chair while you watch T.V. If the bird can explore his immediate area, including you, he will relax. He needs to be assured that being in close contact [with] you is not a threat.

Never hit the bird for any reason. Doing this will undo any progress that you might have made and make future training ten times as difficult.

Let the bird get to know your hand isn't just for grabbing birds. While you sit with him, offer him food and permit him to take it from your hand. Once he will do that, practice letting him climb onto and off of your hand. Place your hand flat in front of him while he is walking, urge him to step onto it and let him walk right off.

Save special food treats for when he is with you. He will, in time, come to trust you, and will gradually quit biting. The hardest part is getting the bird to sit quietly on your hand. If the bird will do that, then you have no problem except your own impatience. Take your time and don't rush it. The more trust you have from your bird the better the relationship will be.

"When I try to take the bird out of his cage he tries to fly back to it . . ."
This is not uncommon. He will naturally want to spend his time in his cage; it is his only place of protection. His food and water is there, and he sleeps there. It is again a matter of trust. With patience, you can get the bird to being happier out of his cage . . . with you, than he is in his cage without you.

Keep the bird with you as much as possible, and do not let him see his cage. . . . Take him in another room and let him [explore] . . . with you right there beside him. Again, T.V. or reading is ideal. You are quiet and still, and he will get braver.

Don't give the bird toys or special food in his cage if he loves it too much already. Save the "special" things for when he is with you. Perhaps having a play-pen that can sit next to you on the couch where he can find interesting things to chew on or eat, will make him look forward to the times when he is out of his cage. Pin a large safety pin (the kind used on horse-blankets) on your clothes and let him play with it. Divert his attention . . . to something interesting. Put a seed in your hand and close it. Let him find the seed. Give him a feather to play with, perhaps a little piece of wood. Just make [this] time out of the cage interesting and relaxing. Soon he will know that life outside is fun. Allow several months and don't rush it.

"I want to have two birds. Can I do that and still have both of them tame?"

Of course, putting birds together can work . . . if you know how to handle it . . .

Keep the training equal with both birds, and work them one at a time. If you have one bird out for a few minutes, take the other bird out as soon as you put the first one back in the cage. Give them equal time.

There are many birds that are pair-bonded, and still like their owners just as much. Spend time with them both. If one bird seems aggressive and objects to the other bird being handled, take the aggressive bird out first. Pecking order is worked out between birds, and you will not be able to change it.

There are three rules to follow in taming, and these cannot be ignored.

1.) Never hit or hurt the bird.
2.) Spend time with them every day (even if it's just five minutes).
3.) Reward good actions with food.

Above all, be patient. Remember, birds live many years. You are developing a friendship that will be expected to last a long time, so give it all the help that you can.

Bill Marcus, "Taming Parrots: Questions and Answers," *Bird World*, August–September 1979, p. 17. Reprinted with the permission of the publisher.

Saving Wild Baby Birds

During the spring and summer months, many people discover lost baby birds that have fallen out of their nest and require immediate attention. If you do find a little orphan, and out of the goodness of your heart decide to take it home with you, then what next? You may wonder how on earth the baby is to be fed, and what? The following article by Katherine Tottenham is a lifesaver, both for you and your little foundling.

– D.A.

There are certain basic principles which apply to the rearing of all young animals. A regular routine, observation of principles of cleanliness, and provision of digestible nutrient material are equally important, but, although normally mammals of any species will instinctively suck to obtain nourishment, young birds will feed only if the correct stimulus is given. For this reason, raising orphan birds is sometimes very difficult.

The main difficulty arises from the common assumption that a young bird should be fed by forcing morsels into its beak – a practice that increases the bird's fear amid unfamiliar surroundings and reduces its chances of survival. Success depends on voluntary food intake, triggered by the manner in which the food is offered. Finding the correct method may be a matter of trial and error, and in such a case each action must be a concise one so that when the bird reacts the stimulus is known and the correct procedure may be adopted in future attempts.

TYPES OF YOUNG BIRDS BASED ON CONDITION AT HATCHING

Young birds are of two main types: nidicolous chicks, which hatch at an early stage of development and are generally blind, helpless, and more or less naked (nestlings); the second type, nidifugous chicks, have a longer incubation period; they leave the shell clad in down feathers and have the ability to run about and pick up food for themselves. Chicks of both types require warmth, but this is all they have in common.

MANAGEMENT OF NIDICOLOUS CHICKS

Nidicolous chicks include all passerine birds, the parrot family, swallows, birds of prey, and kingfishers. These may be grouped on the basis of their usual diet, as seed-eaters, insectivores, and carnivores.

The situation with seed-eaters is unlike that of other species with more obvious dietary demands. In most cases, the chicks are naturally fed on insects until the beak hardens sufficiently to allow the bird to husk seeds for itself. Finches and buntings are in this category and, except for parrots, most birds that crack seeds will require a proportion of insects in their food at the chick stage. Clearly then, if the species of a helpless orphan nestling is in doubt, no harm will be done if it is fed on insects or an equivalent food.

● ● ●

Feeding

The majority of young birds "freeze"' at unaccustomed sights or sounds, and in this state they obviously will refuse to accept food, but quietness and steady movements will do much to prevent fright.

The initial feed is the most difficult. Once a young bird has taken food, it is likely to feed readily at each subsequent meal, but at first extreme patience may be needed. There are nestlings which feed the instant the beak is touched, but these are few; consequently, when the first touch has failed to stimulate feeding, the only thing to do is to follow a series of movements until the right one is discovered. Touch the beak at the tip, on the sides, and at the base where it joins the head, then the chin, the crown of the head, and the back of the body at the shoulders, and finally the sides of the nest as if a parent bird were alighting there. If the chick's eyes are open it may respond to food raised and lowered in front of the beak. If this series of movements fails, try the movements again until the bird gapes, however slightly, and then insert the food into its beak at once.

For small birds the best feeder is a thin, roundtipped wooden spatula cut from a match stick, as this allows the food to be pushed to the back of the bird's tongue and the entrance to the gullet. It is important not to clog the mouth with food, as this may block the windpipe and cause suffocation.

All young passerine birds gape for food, which the parents place right in the gullet. If the species of a nestling is not known, then the presence of "lips" at the sides of the beak will confirm that it is a gaping type. These lips shrivel when the bird becomes self-supporting.

Mynah birds that are to be taught to talk are usually purchased at the gaping stage, but these are easily managed as they are tame and ready to take food from anyone.

The amount of food to give is sometimes a problem; it is generally safe to continue feeding until the bird ceases to gape. Hand-raised young birds are more likely to die of starvation than of a surfeit of food, because the rate of digestion is so fast. As an example, a young mynah bird fed on blackberries passed purple-coloured faeces three minutes later.

The chicks of seed-eating species may be fed on a proportion of commercial rearing food intended for canaries. This is made from dried egg and biscuit meal and forms a good staple diet, to which small insects and larvae and freshly prepared cooked eggs should be added.

Insectivorous birds of the passerine group have gaping chicks which require quantities of live food. Small species, such as warblers, will thrive on maggots, fruit flies, and netted insects. An important point in feeding live foods is that the creature must be killed before it is given to a chick – adult birds will be seen to kill insects before taking them to the nest – and this may be done by pinching the heads of larvae and flies with forceps. The same instrument can be used on earthworms to pinch the body along its length. Fresh but dead food is needed, because if a chick swallows a wriggling animal it is likely to die itself.

Fledgling insectivores will learn to eat insectile mixtures sold for cage birds if some of their accustomed fresh food is placed over it in the dish.

Feeding of Nestling Pigeons and Doves

Nestling pigeons and doves feed naturally by thrusting their soft, pliable beak into the parent's gullet to drink a gruel-like liquid secreted from the lining of the adult bird's crop. Such chicks present great difficulty when being raised by hand because they will never accept offered food.

There are two alternative methods for solving this problem: the bird may be trained to drink a milky fluid from a small vessel, such as an egg cup, or it can be force-fed. This is the only situation in which force pays, as it is simpler and surer; but efforts to establish feeding by the first method are worth while if a very tame bird is desired.

Force-feeding involves prying open the chick's beak between finger and thumb and inserting pellets of bread soaked in creamy milk well down the gullet with the forefinger of the other hand. The bread should be thoroughly soaked but not dripping milk, as the liquid could enter the trachea and cause drowning.

This system prevents the bird from indicating when it has had enough, making the only guide the condition of the crop. It should be well filled but by no means taut; the condition of the crop will also act as a guide to the frequency of feeding, as when it begins to sag another feeding is due.

Pigeons and doves very quickly acquire the plumage necessary for flight, and grow at an equal rate, so that they soon need additional foods in the form of soaked corn (maize) and maple peas, various berries, and green garden peas of a size suited to the species. The beak gradually hardens, and the bird begins to pick up corn for itself when it is about a month old.

In all cases involving the use of fingers for hand-feeding it is important to be sure that the hands are clean and the nails pared smoothly, because damage to the delicate membranes of the chick's mouth or throat may result in inflammation followed by infection.

● ● ●

Feeding of Birds of Prey

Birds of prey bring whole animals to the nest and there rip them up, giving small pieces to the young from their beaks. An owl or hawk chick will often feed if a mouse or bird is dismembered in front of it, but should this procedure fail it will almost certainly accept meat that is raised and lowered slowly a few inches from its face, leaning forward to take the food which should then be pushed gently into the side of the hooked beak.

These birds are equipped with sensitive bristle-like feathers on each side of the beak, and a weak specimen that fails to respond to visual temptation will bite at small pieces of meat rubbed gently across the tips of the bristles.

Once they have begun to feed, the chicks will call when they are hungry. They require about six small meals a day at first, and then graduate to consuming larger chunks at longer intervals.

Young birds of prey alter their mode of accepting food when they are about 4 weeks old, refusing it in the beak but taking pieces placed in the talons. At this age they may be given small mice whole and larger pieces of other animals, until they gain enough strength to tear up dead sparrows, mice, and chicken or rabbit heads. A young eagle or vulture will tackle sheep heads.

Birds of prey regurgitate pellets of indigestible matter, such as bones and feathers, in the normal course of digesting their natural foods, and it is often assumed that roughage must be given to young owls and hawks if they are to thrive. This is not necessary, and such action may even be the cause of so many failures in hand-rearing of these birds. Plenty of flesh food is the important point, and if this consists of mice and sparrows so much the better, but strips of beef steak will be just as nourishing for a fastgrowing chick.

Carnivores are liable to suffer from thirst and as water cannot be given until the bird is capable of drinking from a dish, part of the meat in each meal should be dipped in water immediately before it is offered.

Young birds of prey do not need a heated cage in normal summer weather.

Feeding of Kingfishers

Kingfishers feed their young on small whole fish. Guppies form an ideal food for hand-raised chicks, but a daunting number is required daily to satisfy these birds, which will take up to six an hour from dawn until dusk. No alternative diet has proved successful.

MANAGEMENT OF NIDIFUGOUS CHICKS

The management of young birds that hatch as fluffy chicks, able to run about as soon as they are dry, differs from that of nidicolous species. Apart from a few exceptions, nidifugous chicks are of two kinds: those that are self-feeding and those that take food which is dangled from a parent bird's beak.

Nutritional and Other Needs

The first group includes pheasants, partridges, quail, ducklings, and goslings, all of which will feed from a trough on foods manufactured for young poultry. Game chicks will eat a crumb feed intended for turkey chicks but require some live food in the form of maggots as well; they should also have access to a turf, as scratching gives them strengthening exercise and they obtain grit from the earth adhering to their feet.

Water is essential, but this must be supplied in a way that prevents the chicks from getting wet. The old-fashioned inverted jampot drinker is as good as anything for the purpose.

Sometimes pheasants and other chicks will not feed, but this problem is usually solved by sprinkling eye-catching maggots on the dry food and prodding among the food with a forefinger. If this method fails, the alternative is to introduce, as a "teacher," a farmyard chick of the same age.

Young wildfowl can be managed similarly, but they may be given chicken crumb feed, which has a lower protein content than the turkey crumb feed. Goslings will thrive on a finely pelleted chicken feed. The smaller ducks, like wood ducks, need a proportion of live food, such as maggots, and a ration of chopped lettuce or juicy waterweed.

Water birds that are deprived of their natural mother lack sufficient oil in their plumage to render them waterproof, and so they must be prevented from bathing, let alone swimming. At the same time, because it is essential for them to be able to immerse their heads in water at least once a day if the eyes are not to become inflamed, the best water container is a narrow trough of suitable depth.

Water birds should be handled as little as possible, as disturbance of the plumage retards waterproofing and development of buoyancy.

Self-feeding chicks are comparatively easy to manage for, if they are provided with a source of heat and supplies of food and water, they can be left without attention for a day if necessary. This is not true of beaked nidifugous chicks, which require constant care. Examples of this type of chick are gallinules and rails, species that are difficult to rear without extreme patience and a good measure of luck.

Parent birds of these species feed their young by offering morsels of insects, seeds, and weeds dangling from the beak, which the young bird takes for itself. This method can be simulated by holding such morsels with tapering, round-tipped forceps, which should be moved gently up and down in imitation of the bobbing of a bird's head. These chicks need feeding at least once an hour, but otherwise they will thrive under the same conditions as game birds and wildfowl.

Young gulls are occasionally orphaned and may be reared by beak-feeding with a mush made from flaked raw fish, a teaspoonful of cod liver oil, bread, and enough milk to make a wet but not sloppy mixture.

In all cases where hand-feeding is necessary, an obvious point is sometimes forgotten: the parent bird is bigger than the chick, and so a chick will expect food to be presented from an angle above its head. Finally, some young birds will ignore every method of presenting food and then respond surprisingly to a human attempt, however, ludicrous, at imitating the adult bird's call.

Katherine Tottenham, "Orphan Birds," in *Diseases of Cage and Aviary Birds*, ed. Margaret L. Petrak, V.M.D. (Philadelphia: Lea & Febiger, 1969), pp. 169–74.

Housing Young Orphan Birds

Find a warm dry place in which to keep the baby bird. Even if the enclosure you provide is only temporary, it should be clean, tranquil and large enough to accommodate the particular species.

Featherless or naked babies should be kept warm at 37°C (98.6°F), and those that have some feathers (fledglings) should be kept at 29°C (85°F). A heating pad can be formed into a nest shape and lined with some absorbent material, such as facial tissue or paper towelling, which can be changed frequently. Water should be placed in the cage or enclosure where the bird cannot reach it; this water becomes a source of humidity and prevents the bird from dehydrating. The cage must be large enough to hold these things comfortably, and still remain humid.

Saving Their Lives

Thousands of birds are killed or badly injured every year when they fly into glass windows on buildings. Most people fail to realize that a large plate window in a house looks much different when viewed from outside. The glass reflects the images of trees and sky, and appears to be a continuation of the outdoors. The bird focuses its eyes on the reflected image, and not the glass. These injuries and deaths can be greatly reduced by a simple act of kindness on your part: Place some object on the glass itself, or hang something in front of the glass. It does not matter what the object is, as long as the birds can see it. This will distract the bird's eyes from the reflected image to the glass itself, and give the bird those few precious seconds it needs to veer aside.

Injuries to wild birds are caused by many things, but these collisions with glass are the most common. Cats will also cause injuries because they are natural hunters, waiting in ambush for hours until an unsuspecting bird comes along. If the owner of the cat is quick enough, and the damage is not too great, the bird may be saved.

In many cases, the victims of a window collision are simply stunned, or have had "the wind knocked out of them". These birds should be confined in a dark place that is warmed up to 26°–29°C (80–85°F); this can be accomplished quite easily with a cardboard box placed on a heating pad. Put a thermometer inside the box, so that the temperature can be monitored. After a few hours the bird may revive enough that it can be released again.

All rescued birds should be examined to make sure that nothing is broken. If a fracture is suspected, the bird will need a veterinarian. Some fractures can be mended with a simple splint, others will require surgical repair, and in some cases the leg or wing may have to be amputated due to severe tissue damage. But if someone is willing to look after the bird and keep it as a pet, these amputees can live a happy life.

Do not be tempted to give a wild bird medications that have been purchased indiscriminately. Medications should only be given under the direct supervision of a veterinarian who knows birds. Antibiotics administered in improper doses or given for the wrong reason may do more harm than good. Wait for a proper diagnosis to be made before any treatment is started.

Releasing the Bird

Baby wild birds should only be adopted and hand-reared if the natural parents are no longer able to care for them. No matter how fine the effort, human rearing is second best to a natural upbringing. If there is a good chance the bird will be released to the wild again, try not to tame the bird too much or compromise its native independence. Although it is very tempting to make a pet out of an injured bird, you must keep reminding yourself that the bird is wild and belongs in the wild.

Once the bird has learned to eat on its own and look after itself, every effort should be made to return the bird to its natural environment. It should be released where food is plentiful, so that the transition from its adopted home environment back to the wild is as free as possible from hardship.

Before releasing the bird, try to assess its adaptability. If it is handicapped or at all disabled, it should not be freed. Such birds will not survive in the wild. Similarly, a bird that is too tame and too "people oriented" can neither relate to its own species nor successfully compete with them. An overly tame bird that has no fear of people, dogs, and cats will never survive in nature unless they learn fear. Of course, the bird will also have to master the skill of flying before it can be set free. The skill is learned quickly enough if you give the bird an opportunity to fly about within your home.

When the bird is ready to be released, let it be in good weather, in a place where there are other immature birds of its own kind, even if this means you must drive out into the country to set your wild bird free.

– D.A.

References

Arnall, L. and I.F. Keymer. *Bird Diseases.* Neptune City, N.J.: T.F.H. Publications, Inc., 1975. (528 pp.)

Bates, H. and R. Busenbark. *Guide To Mynahs.* Neptune City, N.J.: T.F.H. Publications, Inc., 1966. (96 pp.)

——. *Introduction to Finches and Softbill Birds.* Neptune City, N.J.: T.F.H. Publications Inc., 1968, (96 pp.)

——. *Finches and Softbilled Birds.* Neptune City, N.J.: T.F.H. Publications, Inc., 1970. (735 pp.)

Bates, H. & R. Busenbark and Dr. Matthew M. Vriends. *Parrots and Related Birds.* 3rd ed. Neptune City, N.J.: T.F.H. Publications, Inc., 1978. (543 pp.)

Forshaw, Joseph M. *Parrots of The World*, Melbourne, New York, London: Lansdowne Editions, 1978, second edition. (616 pp.)

——. *Australian Parrots*, Melbourne, New York, London: Lansdowne Editions, 1981, second edition, (312 pp.)

Fowler, Murray E., D.V.M. *Zoo and Wild Animal Medicine*, Philadelphia, London, Toronto: W.B. Saunders Company, 1978. (151–394 pp.)

Harrison, Greg J., D.V.M. President, *Research Centre for Avian Medicine, Nutrition and Reproduction*, Lake Worth, Florida. Personal Communications.

Hart, Ernest H. *Budgies . . . In Color.* Neptune City, N.J.: T.F.H. Publications, Inc., 1974. (32 pp.)

Kirk, Robert W., D.V.M. *Current Veterinary Therapy VI: Small Animal Practice.* Toronto: W.B. Saunders Co., 1977.

——. *Current Veterinary Therapy VII: Small Animal Practice.* Toronto: W.B. Saunders Co., 1980.

——. *Current Veterinary Therapy VIII: Small Animal Practice.* Toronto, London, Philadelphia: W.B. Saunders Co., 1983, pp. 606–651.

Kirschmann, John D. *Nutrition Almanac.* New York: McGraw-Hill, 1975. (263 pp.)

Lafeber, T.J., D.V.M. *Tender Loving Care For Pet Birds.* Niles, Illinois: Dorothy Products Ltd., 1977. (113 pp.)

Newby, Cliff. *Canaries for Fun and Profit.* Neptune City, N.J.: T.F.H. Publications, Inc., 1965. (64 pp.)

Petrak, Margaret L., V.M.D. *Diseases of Cage and Aviary Birds.* Philadelphia: Lea & Febiger, 1969. (528 pp.)

——. *Diseases of Cage and Aviary Birds*, Philadelphia: Lea & Febiger, 1982, second edition. (680 pp.)

Plath, Karl and Malcolm Davis. *This Is The Parrot.* Neptune City, N.J.: T.F.H. Publications, Inc., 1971. (192 pp.)

Price, Eleanor Avery. *Chicks As Pets.* Neptune City, N.J.: T.F.H. Publications, Inc., 1959. (18 pp.)

Roberts, Mervin F. *How To Train and Raise Pigeons.* Neptune City, N.J.: T.F.H. Publications, Inc., 1962. (64 pp.)

Seal, U.S., et al. *Isis Avian Taxonomic Directory.* 2 Vols. Apple Valley, Minnesota: International Species Inventory System, Minnesota Zoological Garden, 1976.

Stoodley, John and Pat. *Parrot Production, Incorporating Incubation*, Portsmouth, PO8 OSW, England: Bezels Publications, 1983. (108 pp.)

Stroud, Robert. *Stroud's Digest On The Diseases Of Birds.* Neptune City, N.J.: T.F.H. Publications, Inc., 1964. (483 pp.)

Teitler, Risa. *Training African Grey Parrots.* Neptune City, N.J.: T.F.H. Publications, Inc., 1979. (93 pp.)

Veterinary Clinics of North America, Small Animal Practice. Multiple authors, Toronto: W.B. Saunders Co., Vol. 3, Number 2, May 1973. (pp. 143–236).

Veterinary Clinics of North America, Small Animal Practice. Toronto: W.B. Saunders Co., Vol. 9, No. 3, 1979. (pp. 499–568.)

Index

Figures in bold refer to colour plates.